David Heywood is Director of Pastc
Cuddesdon. He has served in parish
south London and the Potteries. Befoiᴄ ᴏᴦᴅᴉᴎᴀtion, he trained as a
teacher and taught for three years in Luton, Bedfordshire. He has
a doctorate in theology and education from Durham University,
in which his main focus was on the way Christians learn and grow
in their faith. He is the author of *Reimagining Ministry*, published in
2011. David is married to Meg, who is chaplain to the Oxford Ministry
Course, and they have four adult children.

SPCK Library of Ministry

Being a Chaplain
Miranda Threlfall-Holmes and Mark Newitt

Community and Ministry: An introduction to community
development in a Christian context
Paul Ballard and Lesley Husselbee

Developing in Ministry: A handbook for effective Christian
learning and training
Neil Evans

Finding Your Leadership Style: A guide for ministers
Keith Lamdin

How to Make Great Appointments in the Church:
Calling, Competence and Chemistry
Claire Pedrick and Su Blanch

Pioneer Ministry and Fresh Expressions of Church
Angela Shier-Jones

Reader Ministry Explored
Cathy Rowling and Paula Gooder

Reflective Caring: Imaginative listening to pastoral experience
Bob Whorton

Skills for Collaborative Ministry
Sally Nash, Jo Pimlott and Paul Nash

Supporting Dying Children and their Families:
A handbook for Christian ministry
Paul Nash

Supporting New Ministers in the Local Church: A handbook
Keith Lamdin and David Tilley

Tools for Reflective Ministry
Sally Nash and Paul Nash

Transforming Preaching: The sermon as a channel for God's word
David Heywood

Youth Ministry: A multi-faceted approach
Sally Nash

TRANSFORMING PREACHING

The sermon as a channel for God's word

SPCK Library of Ministry

DAVID HEYWOOD

First published in Great Britain in 2013

Society for Promoting Christian Knowledge
36 Causton Street
London SW1P 4ST
www.spckpublishing.co.uk

British Library Cataloguing-in-Publication Data
A catalogue record for this book is available from the British Library

ISBN 978–0–281–06341–3
eBook ISBN 978–0–281–07055–8

Typeset by Graphicraft Limited, Hong Kong
First printed in Great Britain by Ashford Colour Press
Subsequently digitally printed in Great Britain

Produced on paper from sustainable forests

Contents

Introduction   vii

1 **Why preach?**   1
   The challenge of preaching   1
   A microcosm of ministry   5
   Preaching for transformation   13
   The word of God   22

2 **The sermon as learning event**   32
   Listening   32
   Remembering   40
   Learning   45
   Learning through reflection   51
   Preaching for learning   54

3 **A step-by-step guide to sermon preparation**   61
   Getting the message   62
   The elements of structure   72
   The varieties of structure   86
   Using visual images   97
   Language to listen to   108
   Getting started   118
   Arriving at a conclusion   129

4 **Involving the congregation**   134
   Interactive preaching   134

Introduction

I was never taught how to preach. My training included the opportunity to preach a sermon in front of a camera and review it, but little else. I have met many in a similar position. The only training we have received in preaching has come first through listening to others and then through trying it ourselves.

I had an advantage over many of my peers. I had been trained as a teacher and had three years' experience of teaching in a secondary school. Preaching is not the same as teaching and a congregation is not the same as a class of 14-year-olds, but I was able to draw on my training and experience as a teacher to help me take my first steps in preaching.

Nowadays the situation is different: almost everyone preparing for the ministry of preaching will receive some kind of training. This book is intended to be used as a resource in that training. But preaching is not something one learns all at once: it is a lifetime's study, and every good preacher knows that he or she has more to learn and that there are ways she or he can improve. So I hope this book will also be useful for preachers with many years' experience, as a reminder, an encouragement, a refresher, or a challenge to try something new.

The literature on preaching is vast: what, then, is the justification for yet another book? There are several reasons why I hope and believe that this book may have a contribution to make. First, over the past 20 years or so we have begun to recognize much more clearly that the local church exists as God's partner in mission. Our understanding of the Church and of Christian ministry is gradually being reshaped by this perception. What then of preaching? How are we to understand the ministry of preaching in the context of Christian mission? It is to this question that the first chapter is directed.

Second, although the literature on preaching is so extensive, there exists almost nothing on the sermon as an event through which people are expected to learn and so to be changed. It is only relatively recently that studies have been undertaken of the ways in which people listen to sermons, what they expect and how much they learn. Over 25 years ago, in his seminal work *Homiletic: Moves and Structures* (1987), David

Buttrick drew on theories about the ways that language and narrative structure our consciousness to make a detailed proposal about the structure of sermons. But even he did not draw upon current work about the way people learn.

Third, although there exists a considerable amount of advice on how to go about preparing a sermon, I have not been able to find this good advice collected in one place. Four or five years ago I set out to create a series of workshops on sermon preparation, drawing largely on two books, Fred Craddock's *Preaching* (1985) and Alvin Rueter's *Making Good Preaching Better* (1997). I have supplemented this with the work of David Day and recently encountered the innovative book by Andy Stanley and Lane Jones, *Communicating for a Change* (2006). What I have attempted to offer is a step-by-step approach that includes all the *necessary* ingredients of a sermon. I don't claim that it includes all the *possible* ingredients. It will be for the reader to judge how far I have succeeded.

Finally, at various periods of my ministry and with particular congregations I have attempted to use interaction as part of the sermon. I embarked on this out of some deep convictions based on my training and experience as a teacher, which call into question the appropriateness of the traditional monologue sermon in any and every situation. Some will consider that this gives the book a rather schizophrenic character: attempting to lay out good practice for the traditional sermon in one chapter and challenging its adequacy in the next. My justification for this is that the Church as a whole is journeying through a period of transition. There are congregations nurtured in traditional ways of thinking and experiencing Christian faith; and there are others seeking to connect with a contemporary culture for which those ways are so alien as to be utterly inaccessible. The challenge to the Church's ministers is to be at home, and to discern appropriate ways of ministry, in both. Naturally, some will be better at one than the other. What I have attempted to do here is to recognize both aspects of this dual task.

Some readers will be using this book in the context of initial training for ordination or lay ministry and may have access to a library. For their sake, I have included suggestions for further reading at the end of each section. As I say in the text, however, preaching is learned primarily through reflecting on practice, and reading should be used as an aid to reflection rather than an end in itself.

I have included very little in the book on delivery, which is a vital aspect of preaching but one in which I am no expert. At Cuddesdon, in addition to the input of our excellent voice coach, we learn about delivery through the risky process of preaching to and receiving feedback from one another. The best brief introduction I know is Geoffrey Stevenson's chapter entitled 'The act of delivery' in Stevenson and Wright (2008).

This book could not have been written without those cohorts of students at Ripon College Cuddesdon whose response to their final-year preaching workshops has helped to sharpen my thinking. Three of them, Paul Chamberlain, Tom Carson and Julia Baldwin (now Julia Pickles), and our vicar at Cuddesdon, Emma Pennington, gave me permission to use extracts from their sermons, and Julia Pickles, Sheena Cleaton and my colleague Keith Beech-Gruneberg each read an earlier draft of the book and made valuable comments. Responsibility for the remaining shortcomings is, of course, entirely my own.

My practice is to write as inclusively as possible by alternating between male and female pronouns. For this reason, the representative preacher sometimes appears as 'she', at other times 'he'. I hope readers will not find this confusing but I find it preferable to using either 'he or she' or 'they'.

References

David Buttrick, 1987. *Homiletic: Moves and Structures*. Minneapolis, Minnesota: Augsburg Fortress Press.

Fred Craddock, 1985. *Preaching*. Nashville, Tennessee: Abingdon Press.

Alvin C. Rueter, 1997. *Making Good Preaching Better*. Collegeville, Minnesota: Liturgical Press.

Andy Stanley and Lane Jones, 2006. *Communicating for a Change*. Colorado Springs, Colorado: Multnomah Books.

Geoffrey Stevenson and Stephen Wright, eds, 2008. *Preaching with Humanity*. London: Church House Publishing.

1

Why preach?

The challenge of preaching

Preaching is characteristic of the life of the Church. An expectation that the worship of the gathered Christian congregation will include a sermon can be traced back at least to the second century in the writings of Justin Martyr. Before that the New Testament testifies to the importance of preaching and teaching as an element in the life of the earliest church and Jesus himself was clearly identified by his contemporaries as a 'rabbi' or teacher.

In my denomination, the Church of England, a sermon is a mandatory element in Sunday worship, whether this takes the form of a 'Service of the Word' or Holy Communion. Moreover, it is an expected part of both the funeral and marriage services, even where few of the congregation can be expected to be regular churchgoers.

And yet, taking the country as a whole, despite an almost universal acceptance of preaching there is considerable variety of practice. In some churches preaching takes centre stage: the sermon is the central act of worship, often lasting as long as an hour. In others it can appear much less important, with congregations growing restless after five or ten minutes. In some circles a particular method of preaching, very often the expository sermon, is approved; in others greater variety is not only tolerated but expected.

Such a variety of practice suggests that the role of the sermon in any given congregation may be a reflection more of tradition than of conviction. Preachers may be responding to the expectations of their congregations, or their denomination or church grouping, rather than basing their practice on a settled, thought-out conviction about the way preaching can best enable and resource Christian discipleship and service. The purpose of this book is not to recommend a standard length of sermon or argue for a particular tradition of worship. It is to help preachers in any and every tradition to understand as clearly as possible what God intends to accomplish through preaching and to provide resources to help them reflect on and improve their practice.

The sermon in its various forms is so much a part of normal Christian experience that it is easy to overlook the key question: 'Why preach?' This is the question I want to address in the third section of this chapter. Before that, in this section and the next, we will look briefly and by way of introduction at preaching in the contexts of contemporary culture and the Church's life and worship.

In contrast to its near-universal acceptance in the Church, in contemporary culture there is considerable doubt about the validity of preaching. The words 'preaching' and 'sermon' are commonly used in a derogatory way to suggest that someone is overstepping their authority or attempting persuasion in an underhand way. To claim authority for a particular point of view is often seen as an illegitimate exercise of power. The right to speak without interruption for a period of between 10 and 40 minutes is seen as archaic.

But it is easy to overestimate the persuasiveness of this line of criticism. The sermon is not the only context in which uninterrupted speech is an accepted norm. Others include the academic lecture, business presentation or political address. These share certain characteristics: the speaker derives his authority from the relevant organization or institution; the listeners recognize this authority, give the speaker their critical attention, but are open to learn or to be persuaded.

In a similar way, preacher and congregation stand together under the authority of Scripture and Christian tradition. The preacher has usually been licensed by the wider Church, entrusted with the authority to interpret and apply Scripture for the present day. And both preacher and congregation share, even if only implicitly, the expectation that God is present in the event of preaching.

Research on what regular churchgoers expect from the sermon emphasizes the vital importance placed on this event of attending to God's word together. In a pilot survey in 2009 researchers in Durham found that no fewer than 96 per cent of respondents 'frequently' or 'sometimes' look forward to the sermon, expecting it to challenge (77.4 per cent), encourage (74.2 per cent), motivate (66.8 per cent) and educate (44.7 per cent) them. A few years previously a more wide-ranging survey was carried out by Christian Theological Seminary, Indianapolis, USA, involving 263 lay people in 28 different congregations.

Here too the researchers found a very high value placed on preaching, along with the expectation that preachers should both challenge and motivate, not being afraid to tackle difficult and controversial topics. In both countries application of the Bible to the problems of everyday life was seen as the bread and butter of preaching.

Another feature of contemporary culture is the vast range of the media of communication with which we are familiar and the way this increasing diversity has begun to reshape the ways in which we relate with each other. Over the last 50 to 100 years the telephone and telegraph have broken down distance, television and the internet have increased the power of the visual, and email and social networking have made interpersonal contact nearly instantaneous. It would be easy to conclude that this media revolution has made face-to-face oral communication obsolete. But again, this would be to overstate the case. In contemporary culture the traditional media of the spoken word and printed page carry different meanings from those they once did, but this does not mean that they are redundant.

Several characteristic features of the sermon in fact help to create a distinctive 'ethos' that is absent in many other forms of communication:

- The sermon is given in context of worship with its focus on the reality of God.
- The presence of a gathered congregation makes this a shared or corporate experience.
- In the case of a normal Sunday service the congregation is bound by a shared faith, in the case of a wedding or funeral by the shared event.
- Sermons both assume and express a relationship between preacher and congregation.
- They involve 'warm' and personal elements such as gesture and tone of voice.

It is also possible to see these distinctive features as expressions of Christian theology. Christians believe in a God who is Father, Son and Holy Spirit, three persons in a relationship of love. We believe that in Jesus God came alongside us as a human being, sharing our experience. As person-to-person communication within a congregation committed to loving and serving one another and the world around, the sermon echoes these elements of distinctively Christian understanding. The challenge to the preacher is to understand not only how the sermon fits into the media culture of today but also how Christian faith critiques that culture. The better we can do this, the better equipped we will be to make the most of its potential.

Another context we need to understand as well as possible is the educational. For many years education has consisted of far more than teacher talk. Teachers are taught and encouraged to use as much variety as possible in their lessons. Children are taught to be self-directed learners, able to define their own learning objectives and draw on a variety of resources to achieve them. Studies of adult learning recognize the importance to adults of being able to set their own goals, work together with others, relate new learning to their existing experience and evaluate their own learning.

The churches have made a start in engaging with the contemporary culture of education but there is still some way to go. When the notes to the liturgy for Holy Communion in the Church of England's *Common Worship* concede that 'The sermon may on occasion include less formal exposition of Scripture, the use of drama, interviews, discussion and audio-visual aids', this is not pandering to a desire for entertainment so much as recognizing the possibility of variety. Even John Stott, who was a trenchant defender of the value of traditional expository preaching, wrote approvingly in *I Believe in Preaching* of one preacher's experiment with a degree of interaction in the sermon. If as preachers we hope that people will listen, learn and remember our sermons, it is important that we know *how* people listen, learn and remember what they hear.

The sermon remains an expected part of Christian worship and preaching a vital part of ministry. And the reason for this is not simply the power of tradition. Most hearers still expect and hope for an encounter with God that will change and direct their lives. The New Testament expresses a basic Christian conviction about the power of God's word to convert and shape the life of both the church and individual believers, and of the place of men and women commissioned by God to play their part in the communication of this word. The call to preach places us under authority, with the responsibility to use the sermon the best we can as the vehicle of God's life-giving word.

Exercise 1A

Recall a sermon, or if possible several sermons, that have spoken powerfully to you and perhaps made a difference in your life. In each case, what were the reasons for this?

- The sermon provided a new perspective on something in the Bible, being a Christian, or daily life.
- The sermon provided new confidence, crystallizing something you already believed.
- The sermon explained something you had previously been puzzling over.
- The sermon inspired you with a new intention.
- There was a combination of these.
- Or some other reason . . .

Further reading

Ronald J. Allen, 2004. *Hearing the Sermon: Relationship, Content, Feeling.* Atlanta, Georgia: Chalice Press.

Rosalind Brown, 2009. *Can Words Express our Wonder?* Norwich: Canterbury Press, Chapter 2: 'The Church's preaching in the past'.

Shane Hipps, 2005. *The Hidden Power of Electronic Culture: How media shape faith, the gospel and the Church.* Grand Rapids, Michigan: Zondervan.

Jolyon Mitchell, 2005. 'Preaching pictures', in David Day, Jeff Astley and Leslie J. Francis, eds, *A Reader on Preaching.* Farnham: Ashgate.

Mary Mulligan and Ronald J. Allen, 2005. *Make the Word Come Alive: Lessons from Laity.* Atlanta, Georgia: Chalice Press.

Mary Mulligan et al., 2005. *Believing in Preaching: What Listeners Hear in Sermons.* Atlanta, Georgia: Chalice Press.

Jenny Rogers, 2007. *Adults Learning*, 5th edition. Buckingham: Open University Press.

John Stott, 1982. *I Believe in Preaching.* London: Hodder and Stoughton, Chapter 1: 'The glory of preaching: a historical sketch'.

Stephen I. Wright, 2010. *Alive to the Word.* London: SCM Press, Chapter 1: 'The historical phenomenon of preaching'.

A microcosm of ministry

At the heart of the Church's worship and life is the expectation that people will encounter God, and preaching is the activity that focuses and expresses this expectation. Karl Barth called it the 'representative event at the centre of the Church's life' (1969, p. 70). But this affirmation also reminds us that preaching takes place in a wider context. It affects and is affected by every other element of the Church's life and ministry:

- *Worship* The sermon typically takes place in the context of worship. To a greater or lesser extent it will be shaped by that worship and the preacher needs to be aware in her preparation of the way the Word of God is proclaimed in those parts of the liturgy that frame the sermon. The liturgy itself, whether formal or informal, proclaims God's character, his grace and love; invites the congregation to penitence for their sins; offers the opportunity for intercession for the world; and at Communion proclaims and invites us to participate in Jesus' saving death and resurrection. At a wedding the sermon is preceded by a lengthy introduction on the Christian understanding of marriage which is echoed in the form of the vows. At a funeral the liturgy provides a framework for the expression of grief and proclaims the Christian hope of resurrection.

  Second, the sermon contributes to the worship. Its emphases may be reflected in the prayers or the music chosen. Its proclamation of the character of God invites a personal and congregational response.

  All of which means that in a very real sense the sermon itself *is* worship: it should be an offering of oneself that glorifies God, enlarges the congregation's understanding of God and enlarges our hearts towards him and the world.

- *Teaching* The sermon is only one element in a church's teaching programme. Others may include a variety of groups and courses, some offered by the local church itself, others by the wider Church through training programmes, festivals, retreats and special events. But aside from these deliberately planned teaching events, the life and worship of the congregation is part of its teaching programme. The way the minister addresses God in worship, the range of concerns brought to God in prayer, the depth of relationship in the congregation: all these embody an understanding of what Christian faith and discipleship is about, equally or even more powerfully than that conveyed in the sermon.

  Nevertheless, the sermon is a vital part of the church's teaching ministry. Its purpose is to help the congregation to live the Christian life. The preacher will aim not simply to provide information, not simply to help people grow in their understanding of the Bible and Christian doctrine, but to apply these to their life together as a congregation and to their lives in the wider world. The effect of the church's regular preaching should be to enable and encourage God's people in a Christian stance for living: to build an expectation of the new age to come and strengthen the faith and love through which this hope is lived out.

- *Pastoral care* A great deal of pastoral care also takes place through preaching. The sermon may address the duties or transitions of life, such as parenthood or bereavement, providing guidance and encouragement to those encountering them and strengthening the ability of the congregation to support its individual members. It may comment on the life of the congregation, perhaps rebuking sinful tendencies, such as gossip, encouraging mutual forgiveness or teaching the value of each person's uniqueness. Preaching may be used to teach and encourage the value of community over against individualism; it may draw attention to the insidious features of contemporary culture, such as consumerism, that erode love and compassion; it may teach the congregation how to become a community of care.

  Preaching takes place in the context of the relationship between preacher and congregation. The sermon is always an expression of that relationship and may help to deepen it and make it richer. On the other hand, an insensitive sermon may damage it. It is vital, therefore, for preachers to know their congregations as well as possible, to be aware of the situations they encounter day by day and the problems they face.

- *Leadership* Leadership is exercised largely through the way the leader does other things: the way she relates to people, demonstrates her priorities in small decisions, conducts meetings, prays with people and confronts problems. One of those 'other things' will usually be preaching. Sermons can play a vital role in leadership: they may create vision, communicate values, suggest direction and inspire faith and action. Leaders need to beware the temptation to use the sermon slot simply to communicate their particular agenda or, even worse, to berate the church for its lack of response to the leader's vision. On the other hand, preaching is a perfectly legitimate way to present the biblical foundations for important decisions in the church's life.

  In one congregation I led, one of my concerns was to encourage the church to accept children as a vital part of its life and worship. We did this in a number of ways: forming a young people's music group to help lead the worship, organizing regular all-age events, finding opportunities for the young people to play a part in ministry. But alongside this, sermons were a valuable means of explaining the importance Jesus placed on children as part of God's kingdom.

- *Evangelism* It is not necessary for there to be an appeal for a sermon to be evangelistic. Nor does it even have to focus directly on the cross and resurrection. There are occasions when it will be appropriate to challenge commitment or encourage a decision to follow Christ. But any sermon in which the grace and truth of God in Jesus Christ is proclaimed is evangelistic. The word of God has a power of its own to convict and convert. And research shows that conversion is a life-long process: to show the regular congregation how to grow in faithfulness to the gospel may be equally effective in bringing a hesitating newcomer to a sense of its relevance to his life.

For each of us as preachers, one or more of these is likely to be most important. There are a few for whom no sermon is complete without an evangelistic appeal, others for whom aspects of liturgy such as Holy Communion and the Church's year shape their preaching. Some of us are more pastorally minded, others see ourselves primarily as teachers, and others give priority to the sermon's leadership function. In reality, all these elements are present and all play a part in shaping a ministry of preaching. It is therefore valuable to understand the influences that have shaped us: for those of us who have been Christians since childhood, the assumptions about preaching we may have grown up with; for others, the emphasis of the church in which we first became Christians; for all of us, the example of preachers we remember and whose ministry we have valued.

Whatever our inherited assumptions, it is important to recognize that preaching affects and is affected by every other aspect of the church's life. It is a microcosm of ministry. This suggests that it is important that the function of preaching in shaping and forming the life of the congregation be kept continually under review. It may be helpful for all who share the preaching for a particular congregation to think and pray together regularly about the balance of teaching and pastoral care and the direction of leadership expressed through the sermons over a period of time. At the heart of this exercise is listening to God and discerning what he is doing or may want to do in the life of the congregation.

A combination of skills

Not only does preaching bring together all the different aspects of church life, it also requires the integration of a variety of skills, attitudes and personal qualities.

- As preacher you will need to be constantly open to the word of God, accepting the challenge to grow in your faith.
- You will need to be aware of and able to nurture your relationship with the congregation.
- You will need to know how to interpret the Bible, and to keep working to improve your understanding of it.
- You will also need the facility for interpreting culture and society, both the local and the national and international.
- You will need to have worked on your skills in planning and preparing the sermon.
- You will also need to work on your public speaking skills: the use of voice, stance and gesture.

In this respect, learning to preach is rather like learning to drive. To be able to drive you have to learn the Highway Code, master the controls of the car and become alert to the road situation. You also need the qualities of patience and self-control, without which you will not be safe on the road. Only when you can put all these together are you likely to pass your test and become a qualified driver.

In the same way, the ministry of preaching requires a variety of skills and qualities of character. Only when you are able to bring all these together will you be a competent preacher. On the other hand, like driving, it can be done. Each summer in my present post, I send students on a four-week placement in an unfamiliar church, where many of them will preach for the first time. And each summer I receive back sermon evaluations from members of the congregations full of praise for the sermons they have heard. The students are not the finished article but, through modelling themselves on the preachers they have experienced and using their intuition about good communication, they have been able to put together sermons which God has used.

Like driving, we learn preaching from practice. No one becomes a good driver by learning the Highway Code and reading a manual. Driving is learned practically, through experience and reflection. In the same way, no one will become a good preacher simply by reading this or any other book. Preaching is learned by experience and reflection, by evaluating each sermon, as often as possible with the help of others, asking what was good and what could have been better. The purpose of reading books about preaching is to alert you to all

9

that may be important, to act as a reminder of what to aim for or a guide to what may be going wrong. So may I encourage you, having read the book for the first time, to follow up the suggestions for further reading and to revisit sections of this book from time to time, using the exercises for practice, so that you continue to learn and develop in this vital aspect of ministry.

Four principles

In the next section, I want to give a much fuller answer to the question, 'Why preach?' But before doing so, I would like to end these introductory sections by sharing four personal convictions:

- *God is a communicator* God will use every opportunity he is given to speak to people today and your sermons will be such opportunities. The Bible tells us that God is always speaking through his creation, which witnesses to his power and deity. He is present whenever his people gather and his word has a power of its own to bring conviction. This does not absolve us from working on our preaching to make it as effective as possible, but it does mean that in the end its effectiveness does not depend entirely on us.
- *People really want to hear* The research from Durham and Indianapolis confirms that most existing churchgoers look forward to the sermon for guidance and challenge. This may not apply in quite the same way to people who are not churchgoers. For many people outside the Church, sermons do not have a particularly good reputation: they expect them to be far from memorable and even boring. But even though they may be wary of sermons, many people outside the Church really want to hear from God. They have deep questions about the meaning of life and what comes after it. In a fragmented world, many long for a set of beliefs to bring coherence to their lives and provide the foundation for a satisfying, integrated lifestyle. And many long for help in order to address and work through areas of pain in their lives. If they hear a preacher talking about these in language they can understand and relate to, they are more than likely to be willing to listen.
- *You have all the resources you need* God's ultimate way of revealing himself was through a person, Jesus Christ, the truth and love

of God incarnate. Today God still uses people as his messengers. Though far from perfect, we, as preachers, are still equipped to convey something of God's truth. Wherever God calls, he also equips. He provides us with his Spirit, and asks us to cultivate the ability to listen to him speaking in Scripture and through culture. To be aware of our shortcomings does not disqualify us from preaching; rather, it is an essential part of our preparation.

- *Your life is the most important factor* It has been said that every preacher has just one sermon: her life. We will not be able to speak with conviction unless we ourselves have experienced the truth of what we proclaim. We will not be able to provide leadership through preaching if our character undermines the values we want our congregation to embrace. Our authority as preachers depends on the trust we are able to inspire, and this in turn depends on the authenticity and transparency of our lives and the love and care we have communicated. In its essence, preaching is a relationship: if our sermons are to be believable our lives have to be believable also.

EXERCISE 1B

What would you say were your aims as a preacher? Consider the following possibilities, add any others you wish and then rank them in order of priority:

- To help people to understand the Bible better
- To help people to understand and relate to Christian tradition
- To preach so as to enhance the worship
- To provoke an encounter with God
- To challenge people to live distinctive Christian lives
- To help people to cope with the problems they encounter in their daily lives
- To lead people to conversion to Christian faith
- To promote deeper and more authentic relationships among the congregation
- Others . . .

As you draw up your rank order, consider the influences that have led you to these priorities. Are you satisfied with them, or do you see a need to change?

Exercise 1C

How do you think God communicates with us:

- through Scripture?
- through other people?
- in dreams?
- through circumstances?
- through preaching?
- in creation?
- in particular contexts?
- through the Christian community?
- by means of the Holy Spirit?
- others . . . ?

For each means that you choose, try to work out a *theological* explanation: that is, an explanation that derives from what you believe about God's character and ways of working.

Now rank the means you have chosen in order of importance and give a theological explanation for your ranking.

References

Karl Barth, 1969. *Church Dogmatics*, Volume I.1. Edinburgh: T. and T. Clark.

Further reading

Ronald J. Allen, 2001. *Preaching and Practical Ministry*. Atlanta, Georgia: Chalice Press.

Simon Baker, 2012. 'Preaching for today', in Tim Ling and Lesley Bentley, eds, *Developing Faithful Ministers*. London: SCM Press.

Rosalind Brown, 2009. *Can Words Express our Wonder?* Norwich: Canterbury Press, Chapter 4: 'The calling to preach'; Chapter 7: 'Pastoral and prophetic: the focuses of preaching'.

David Busic, 2003. 'Planning the preaching calendar', in *The Leader's Guide to Effective Preaching*. Kansas City: Beacon Hill Press.

Charles Chadwick and Phillip Tovey, 2001. *Developing Reflective Practice for Preachers*. Grove Worship 164, Cambridge: Grove.

Fred Craddock, 1985. *Preaching*. Nashville, Tennessee: Abingdon Press, Chapter 1: 'Introduction'; Chapter 2: 'The sermon in context'.

Alvin C. Rueter, 1997. *Making Good Preaching Better.* Collegeville, Minnesota: Liturgical Press, Chapter 12: 'The message communicated by the preacher's character'.

Stephen I. Wright, 2010. *Alive to the Word.* London: SCM Press, Chapter 2: 'Contemporary functions of preaching'.

Preaching for transformation

In the previous sections we have looked briefly at preaching in the contexts of contemporary culture and the Church's life and worship. We saw that preaching is related to worship, teaching, pastoral care, leadership and evangelism. All these are important in shaping both particular sermons and our ministry of preaching as a whole. But I want to suggest that there are two other contexts even more important than these. In the second chapter I want to look at the educational context and view the sermon as a learning event. But in this section and the following I want to look at the most important context of all: the place of preaching in the mission of God. It is here, I want to suggest, that we find the answer to the question, 'Why preach?'

The mission of God

'How is it possible,' asks Lesslie Newbigin, 'that the gospel should be credible, that people should come to believe that the power which has the last word in human affairs is represented by a man hanging on a cross? I am suggesting that the only answer, the only hermeneutic of the gospel, is a congregation of men and women who believe it and live by it' (1989, p. 227). In this way Newbigin expresses his conviction that the life of the local congregation plays a central role in the Church's missionary endeavour. The local church is Christ's body, his embodied presence for their particular locality or network of relationships. As such it is God's chosen partner in mission, called, in Newbigin's words, to be a 'foretaste, sign and agent of the kingdom' (2006, pp. 138–9).

For centuries the Church has been embedded in the British way of life. Its culture has both helped to shape and been shaped by the culture of British society. But this very visibility has to some extent prevented us from recognizing the considerable areas of society and culture where the Church has been marginal or even absent: for example, large parts of our great cities as they grew up rapidly in the nineteenth century and, in the twenty-first century, networks of younger people for whom religion in general and Christianity in particular appear a curious survival from an irrelevant past. It has also tended to obscure questions of the origins and purpose of the Church: how did it arise and why does it exist? But when these questions are asked, the answers are very clear: the Church arose in response to God's mission in the world and its calling and purpose is to play its part in that mission.

'The church,' writes Martyn Atkins, 'derives its being from the missionary God and is created and shaped to share in the *missio Dei*, whose goal is the kingdom of God' (2008, p. 19). This understanding of the Church's existence and purpose goes deeper than the observation that Christianity took root as the result of the preaching of previous generations. It affirms that the Church owes its life and purpose to the mission of God. It is created by and for mission. In the much-quoted words of Emil Brunner, 'The church exists by mission as a fire exists by burning' (1931, p. 158).

Mission is to be an overflow from the life of the congregation. Not only is the local church called to proclaim Christ through its words and actions, it is called to *be* Christ to the world through its life and fellowship. As a 'foretaste' of the kingdom it should carry in its life a 'flavour' of the kingdom or, as Paul expresses it, the 'aroma of Christ' (2 Corinthians 2.15). The actions by which the local church engages in mission will include evangelism, care for the needy, action to promote justice and a fully human life in national and local community, and care for God's created world. But these actions should not represent an anxious or frenetic activism; rather, they should overflow from the love of God experienced and shared among members of the local congregation. As John V. Taylor writes, 'The gift of the Holy Spirit in the fellowship of the church first enables Christians to *be*, and only as a consequence of that sends them to do and to speak' (1972, p. 134).

The most fundamental reason this is so is that the mission of God is itself an overflow from the life of God the Trinity. The love of Father, Son and Holy Spirit overflows first in the creation and sustaining of the world, then in the sending of Jesus for its redemption, and finally in the sending of the Church in the power of the Holy Spirit to work for the transformation of the world in preparation for the final coming of the kingdom of God. Moreover, the sending of Jesus provides a pattern for the mission of the Church. Jesus took on human form and became a man of his time, embedded in a particular culture and yet pointing beyond it to the kingdom of God. The outward form of his mission consisted of his words and action in the power of the Holy Spirit; its inner reality was his presence and life as the Word incarnate. During the short period of his ministry Jesus took steps to ensure that his mission would continue: he formed a community by whom he would be remembered and worshipped and among whom the quality of his own life was to be evident. It was this community that he commissioned to continue his work.

So Newbigin's insight that the life of the local congregation is the best witness to the truth of the gospel can be seen to arise from the nature of the mission of God itself. But in the context of contemporary society there are other more pragmatic reasons for recognizing its importance. In a pluralistic society, truth is up for grabs. People are aware that they can choose from a variety of religions and philosophies, or 'pic'n'mix' to suit themselves. Institutions like the Church no longer carry the authority they once did because they exist in a competing market. Against this background the claim to possess the truth is often taken as an exercise in power or manipulation. What carries conviction is what works and makes a difference. If the Christian gospel is to be credible people need to see it making a difference in the lives of those who profess it.

Moreover, it is the congregation that is important rather than individuals. It is in the local congregation that Jesus' central command to 'love one another' is to be carried out. As John Taylor points out, the New Testament is full of exhortations to the churches calling attention to their life together: 'love one another', 'accept one another', 'serve one another', 'bear one another's burdens' (1972, p. 126). This is because it is in the quality of our relationships rather than our individual holiness that God is seen. A local church does not present itself as a group of finished saints capable of modelling the good life, but as a congregation of forgiven sinners, the qualification for which is simply to recognize one's own weaknesses and failings. So it is in relationships of mutual care and acceptance that God is most likely to be encountered.

These pragmatic points – the importance of authentic practice and loving relationships – reflect the fundamental truth that Christianity is by its very nature relational and practical. Its primary revelation was given not in the shape of a doctrine or philosophy but through a person, Jesus Christ. Throughout the Bible the concept of 'knowledge' is intensely practical. To 'know' God is to be in a 'formative relationship' with him (Downing, 1964, p. 42). For example, writing to the Colossians Paul prays that they will be 'filled with the knowledge of God's will in all spiritual wisdom and understanding', so that they may 'lead lives worthy of the Lord, fully pleasing to him' (Colossians 1.9–10). Paul's 'so that' conveys purpose as well as expectation: it is not simply that the knowledge of God can be expected to lead to transformed lives but that such transformation is its very purpose. Moreover, Paul appears to envisage a virtuous cycle: knowledge leading to changed lives leading to further knowledge. Its result is not simply that 'you bear fruit in every good work' but also that 'you grow in the knowledge of God'. In fact, the transformation of the congregation lies at the heart of Paul's missionary thinking and of the New Testament as a whole.

So the answer to our question, 'What is the role of preaching in the mission of God?' is this: the purpose of preaching is the transformation of the Church. Its aim is to help the Church to become what it is called to be, the continuation of Christ's mission in the present day.

Transformation

'Preaching,' writes Paul Scott Wilson, 'is an event in which the congregation hears God's word, meets their Saviour, and is transformed through the power of the Holy Spirit to be the kind of community God intends' (2007, p. 5). And Walter Brueggemann writes: 'I understand preaching to be the chance to summon and nurture an alternative community with an alternative identity, vision and vocation, preoccupied with praise and obedience towards the God we Christians know fully in Jesus of Nazareth' (2007, p. 56). The purpose of preaching is transformation: the formation of a congregation as it learns to love in the way Jesus called his followers; and the transformation of its individual members as the understanding of all it means to live under God's rule changes their priorities and guides them towards a lifestyle powerfully distinct from that of the surrounding culture.

For the New Testament the transformation of the Church to become progressively like Jesus takes centre stage. In Romans 8.29 Paul writes: 'Those whom [God] foreknew he also predestined to be conformed to the image of his Son, in order that he might be the firstborn within a large family.' After his lengthy digression on the place of the Jews in God's purposes, Paul returns immediately to this theme. 'Do not be conformed to this world,' he writes, 'but be transformed by the renewing of your minds, so that you may discern what is the will of God' (Romans 12.2). This conformity to the image of Jesus is the *telos*, by which is meant both goal and end point, to which Christians are to aspire. The realization of this goal is called *teleiosis*, best translated as 'maturity'.

We see this first of all in the teaching of both Jesus and the apostles about Christian lifestyle. The Beatitudes in Matthew 5.1–16 present a vision of the blessed or happy life that would be counter-cultural in virtually any culture or historical period because it means embracing the values of humility and sacrifice rather than security and self-assertion. Moreover, this radical break on the part of Jesus' disciples from the world's standards and expectations is to lead to a lifestyle that glorifies the Father as Christians influence the world both secretly, like salt, and openly, like a lamp on a stand.

In the same vein, the 'fruit of the Spirit' listed by Paul in Galatians 5.22–23 point to a set of qualities and resulting lifestyle radically different from the practices that were 'obvious' in the society around them. Paul's appeal to the Galatians is echoed in virtually every one of his letters and those of the other apostles as they urge the believers to 'lead a life worthy of the calling to which you have been called' (Ephesians 4.1).

In some ways it is remarkable that Paul, who was so clear about his personal calling as an evangelist and church planter, should include in his letters no exhortations to his converts to engage in personal evangelism. The closest any of the apostles come to this is Peter's instruction, 'Always be ready to make your defence to anyone who demands from you an account of the hope that is in you' (1 Peter 3.15). Instead, all the New Testament letters go into detail about Christian behaviour. Within the church Christians are to display humility, gentleness, compassion and mutual love. Their roles as husbands and wives, parents and children, masters and slaves were to be governed by an ethic of mutual submission. They are to learn and put into practice the 'mind' of Christ himself, characterized by love, humility and self-sacrifice.

Paul's primary passion for the churches he founded was to see them transformed into the image of Jesus Christ. In Colossians 1.28 and 29 he describes himself and his companions as 'warning everyone and teaching everyone in all wisdom, so that we may present everyone mature (*teleion*) in Christ. For this I toil and struggle,' he continues, 'with all the energy that he powerfully inspires within me.' To the recalcitrant Galatians he describes himself as 'in the pain of childbirth until Christ is formed (*morphothe*) in you' (Galatians 4.19).

This passionate concern comes to its full expression in the letter to the Ephesians, whose author, if not Paul himself, was certainly someone close to him and who knew his mind. The key passage is 4.11–16, where the leadership gifts, apostles, prophets, evangelists, pastors and teachers, are said to be given to equip God's people for the work of ministry and for the upbuilding of the body of Christ,

> until all of us come to the unity of the faith and of the knowledge of the Son of God, to maturity [*eis andra teleion*], to the measure of the full stature of Christ . . . We must grow up in every way into him who is the head, into Christ, from whom the whole body, joined and knitted together . . . as each part is working properly, promotes the body's growth in building itself up in love.

A united, loving church, growing together into the form of Jesus Christ, is the goal for which the apostle works and prays.

In their book *Being a Priest Today* Christopher Cocksworth and Rosalind Brown describe the work of the 'presbyter' as being 'to see that the church grows into its natural form – the priestly body of Christ, a community embodying and demonstrating the *with-other-ness* and *for-other-ness* of God's life of love' (2006, p. 20). The call of the ordained minister is to help the church become all that God intends it to be and preaching is one of the means by which this call is to be fulfilled. Nor is this only the role of the ordained minister: the ministry that builds up the church is rightly shared. Readers, lay preachers and all those called to preach share in this ministry of forming the church into the likeness of Christ, helping it to come to *teleiosis*, that maturity, beauty or perfection that God wills for his people.

Of course, there are occasions where preaching is called for, but the congregation includes or is largely made up of people who would not call themselves members of a local congregation: a wedding, funeral or civic service, for example. Does this view of the purpose of preaching as transformation apply to those occasions or do we need to look for some other purpose? Should our preaching be confined to a celebration of the occasion, or, in the case of a funeral, of the life of the deceased? Or are these occasions for a direct evangelistic appeal?

I believe there is continuity between the transformative purpose of preaching in a local Christian congregation and those other public occasions when preaching is called for, and I think this is recognized by the revisers of the Church of England's liturgy in the decision to make preaching mandatory at weddings and funerals. At the heart of Christian transformation is a vision of human life as God intended it and an offer of the power to live 'life in all its fullness'. The call to lifelong commitment to one another in marriage, the challenge of facing grief and loss, deep questions about the purpose of life and the nature of life after death, are just a few of the questions and challenges we share with people of all faiths and none. In all these areas faith in Christ brings with it a distinctive 'wisdom', a solid foundation on which to build our lives. Many people who do not see themselves as 'religious' nevertheless long for a way of living integrated, ethically satisfying lives. To explore these areas and to share this wisdom is perhaps the most effective kind of evangelism. Thus, when preaching at a wedding, I look for ways of evoking the longing for commitment that many share; the sermon based on the film *Notting Hill* that I share in Chapter 3 was one of those. And at funerals I try to explore aspects of shared everyday life, like work or care for a family, and to offer a Christian perspective on these.

In any case, membership of a local congregation is far from being simply a matter of 'in' or 'out'. 'Belonging' to a local congregation may mean different things to different people. Some will be committed Christians of long standing, playing a central role in the life of the church. Others will be enquirers, putting an occasional toe in the water of faith. Still others, because of the circumstances of their lives, may be mainly receivers of the congregation's love and care. And yet the preacher is entitled to assume, just by their presence in worship, that acceptance of the authority of the institution, critical listening and willingness to learn or to be persuaded that we saw earlier was a characteristic of preaching. Christian transformation is a journey, and in any given congregation the different members will be at a variety of different points on that journey. In a similar way, even on those occasions when the majority of a congregation may be non-believers, there is usually an implicit acceptance of the preacher's role as a representative and spokesman for Christian faith. Their journey of faith may be near its beginning, but we believe that as human beings, created and loved by God, his word nevertheless addresses them. The way the sermon is pitched may be different, but there is continuity between its role on these occasions and in regular Sunday worship.

In addition, as Stephen Wright points out in his insightful book, *Alive to the Word* (2010), there are many occasions on which the Church speaks, through its preaching, to the wider community. With the decline of 'Christendom', in which the Church was an accepted and authoritative institution within the structures of power, come increasing opportunities for the Church to sound a distinctive note in society. Wright suggests the value of the personal and face-to-face in an age of electronic communication; of space for reflection in an increasingly frenetic society; of a word of reconciliation amid a tendency to polarization; the evocation of another and truer world, a divine perspective, the sense of speaking under authority as well as with authority, of a distinctively Christian wisdom. As the spokesperson of a community seeking transformation through obedience, the preacher acts as a prophetic voice in a culture committed to the values of self-assertion and the satisfaction of desire.

Throughout the New Testament the word of God is seen as one of the means through which the transformation of the Christian community into the image of Christ, which is the principal goal of preaching, is accomplished. In Jesus' parable of the sower, the word is described as a seed which, when it falls in good soil, grows and produces fruit. Both James and Peter take up this image. James urges his readers to 'welcome with meekness the implanted word that has the power to save your souls' (James 1.21) and in 1 Peter the apostle reminds his readers that they have been 'born anew, not of perishable but of imperishable seed, through the living and enduring word of God' (1 Peter 1.23). It is important to place this emphasis on the role of the word in its context alongside that of the sacraments and the Holy Spirit. The sacraments are not only a visible and tangible reminder of the work of Christ on our behalf but are real participation in this present age in the life of the new age to come. The Holy Spirit is the spirit of Christ himself, the one who nurtures those qualities in our lives that echo those of Jesus himself. But the word too has a vital part to play and a power of its own to accomplish change. 'The gospel,' writes Paul, 'is the power of God to salvation' (Romans 1.16). What kind of a power is this?

EXERCISE 1D

Consider the following question: As teachers or preachers, is our message to be mainly for individuals or mainly for the church?

Take 10 marks and allocate them between the two according to how important you think each to be. Reflect on the reasons that led you to your answer.

EXERCISE 1E

Read and ponder on the following texts. What does each tell you about God's purpose to transform the Church into the image of Jesus Christ?

- John 1.10–13
- Hebrews 2.10–13
- Romans 8.15–17
- 2 Corinthians 3.17–18
- Colossians 3.1–10
- Ephesians 4.11–16
- 1 John 3.1–3
- 1 Corinthians 13.8–12.

Several of these passages use the image of seeing face to face. Explore the associations this image has for you. What light do these associations throw on the process of transformation?

References

Emil Brunner, 1931. *The Word in the World.* London: SCM Press.

Gerald Downing, 1964. *Has Christianity a Revelation?* London: SCM Press.

Paul Scott Wilson, 2007. *The Practice of Preaching.* Nashville, Tennessee: Abingdon Press.

Further reading

Martyn Atkins, 2008. 'What is the essence of the Church?' in Steven Croft, ed., *Mission-shaped Questions.* London: Church House Publishing.

Dietrich Bonhoeffer, 1959. *The Cost of Discipleship.* London: SCM Press, Part 4: 'The Church of Jesus Christ and the life of discipleship'.

Walter Brueggemann, 2007. 'Preaching as reimagination', in *The Word Militant.* Minneapolis, Minnesota: Fortress Press. Also in David Day, Jeff Astley and Leslie J. Francis, eds, 2005. *A Reader on Preaching.* Farnham: Ashgate.

Christopher Cocksworth and Rosalind Brown, 2006. *Being a Priest Today,* 2nd edition. Norwich: Canterbury Press, Chapter 1: 'Being called'; Chapter 5: 'Being for the word'.

Stephen Cottrell, 2006. *From the Abundance of the Heart: Catholic Evangelism for All Christians.* London: Darton, Longman and Todd.

Steven Croft, 2009. *Jesus' People.* London: Church House Publishing.

David Day, 1998. *A Preaching Workbook.* London: SPCK, Chapter 13: 'Playing squash against a haystack'.

Lesslie Newbigin, 1988. 'On being the church for the world', in Giles Ecclestone, ed., *The Parish Church*. London: Mowbray; also in Paul Weston, ed., 2006. *Lesslie Newbigin: Missionary Theologian*. London: SPCK.

Lesslie Newbigin, 1989. *The Gospel in a Pluralist Society*. London: SPCK.

Roger Standing, 2010. 'Mediated preaching: homiletics in contemporary British culture', in Geoffrey Stevenson, ed., *The Future of Preaching*. London: SCM Press.

Andy Stanley and Lane Jones, 2006. *Communicating for a Change*. Colorado Springs, Colorado: Multnomah Books.

John V. Taylor, 1972. *The Go-Between God: The Holy Spirit and the Christian Mission*. London: SCM Press.

Graham Tomlin, 2002. *The Provocative Church*. London: SPCK.

Stephen I. Wright, 2010. *Alive to the Word*. London: SCM Press.

The word of God

Written words, spoken words

Since the invention of the printing press over 500 years ago the printed word has been the world's dominant form of communication. Once the privilege of a few, reading and writing have become a universal gateway to a world of ideas and information exchanged through scientific papers, academic journals, poetry, novels, newspapers and magazines. Our culture has been conditioned by the characteristics of the printed word.

In our age all this is beginning to change. Our culture is becoming increasingly visual and oral as television makes available a diverse range of visual experience as well as the sound of the spoken word. Email, text and Twitter are changing the character of the written word, making it more informal and spontaneous. And in 2008 the campaigning style of Barack Obama led to speculation that the ancient art of rhetoric might be about to make a comeback.

These changes in the character of the written word remind us that there existed a time before the printing press, the age of the spoken word. This was an age of predominantly oral culture, when comparatively few could read or write and books were the possession of the elite. In Western Europe churches were highly decorated, and the Bible story was conveyed chiefly through wall paintings and stained-glass windows. In oral cultures, even when books exist, experience of words is conditioned not by the written but by the spoken word.

The most important characteristic of the formal written word is information content: even when used to paint a scene in a novel the emphasis is on the information conveyed. The printed word lasts: it remains available for a long period to be checked and compared with other sources. This means that apart from such things as personal letters, the audience for the written word is general and impersonal. A piece of writing may have a particular audience in mind, but that audience consists of many people with a range of interests. A newspaper, article or book can be treated as a resource: readers can take it at their own pace, can go back and refer to it as many times as they choose, may even make notes in the margin or quote it at length in their own writing.

Because of this the invention of printing also had the enormous effect of fuelling the growth of individualism. To be able to read was to be able to interpret the text for oneself. And in the early days of printing it was the reading and study of the Bible that made this most apparent. Instead of a universal Church with an authoritative and unchallengeable interpretation of Christian faith, the availability of the Bible in the language of the people enabled every reader to become his or her own interpreter and gave rise to an increasing diversity of Christian churches and sects.

Because the printed word is fixed there is little or no scope for conversation. In contrast, the spoken word has an immediate interpersonal context. It is spoken by a particular person to specific others at a particular time and place. Spoken words have emotional tone: they may be spoken loudly or softly, calmly or excitedly, passionately or aggressively. They are used to 'do things': to influence or persuade, demand or concede. Although the printed word also has a purpose, to entertain or inform, persuade or convince, the writer lacks the opportunity to engage directly with the audience, to respond, rephrase or clarify. In oral cultures, where dialogue and immediacy are uppermost, experience of words is conditioned by the spoken word, whose most important characteristic is not so much information content as 'performative force', the impact on the hearer.

Spoken words have a group dynamic. The act of speaking to an audience using tone and gesture to convey emotion as well as information, to influence and persuade, creates a shared experience. A relationship is created between speaker and audience; a certain level of trust is engendered. Spoken communication is 'warm' and relational in contrast to the much 'cooler' and more individual experience of the written word.

This contrast between the written and the spoken word means that we have to be careful when using electronic media as a supplement to the spoken word in preaching. It is common in some circles for the preacher to use PowerPoint to emphasize the main headings of an address. As soon as this happens, the written word changes the congregation from a united audience to a collection of individuals and the emphasis is shifted from the intention of the sermon to its information content. If, on the other hand, PowerPoint is used to project images rather than words, the warm, relational aspect of the sermon is preserved and even enhanced. Images speak to the affective and intuitive aspects of our minds, the 'right side of the brain', in contrast to the written word, which tends to make us analytical and individual.

These features of the spoken word remind us of the characteristics of all words, some of which tend to be obscured in a literate culture. Of course words convey information, but they do so in a context of relationship. A word is an action: spoken into the conversation of a few, or designed to be broadcast to many; or written as a contribution to a much more general 'conversation'; but all intended to influence, to change the course of a relationship, to affect the decisions and actions of others. Words do not simply record reality: they create it. They move events forward. They present new and previously undreamed of possibilities. Or they create 'plausibility structures' within which particular beliefs and actions make sense and are justified.

The word of God

In our literary culture, many people are used to thinking of God's word primarily as accurate information. But the Bible, even though written down, was created in an oral culture in which experience of words was conditioned by the spoken word. In fact, our concept of the 'word of God' as primarily information, arising from the assumptions of our culture, is 'unbiblical'. In the Bible, the word of God is primarily an immensely powerful action, both creative and destructive.

This emerges in its very first chapter:

Then God said, 'Let there be light'; and there was light.

(Genesis 1.3)

and in the psalmist's reflection on this action:

> By the word of the LORD the heavens were made,
> and all their host by the breath of his mouth.   (Psalm 33.6)

Here, God's word acts as a powerful cause in the natural world. He is portrayed as an agent with a purpose, and the vehicle of his intention is the spoken word. In the New Testament, where it is made clear that Jesus is the one through whom and for whom all things were created, the writer to the Hebrews tells us that, 'He [Jesus] sustains all things by his powerful word' (Hebrews 1.3).

Moreover the word of God acts as a cause not only in the natural world but in historical time: it brings about events that otherwise would not take place:

> For as the rain and the snow come down from heaven,
> and do not return there until they have watered the earth,
> making it bring forth and sprout,
> giving seed to the sower and bread to the eater,
> so shall my word be that goes out from my mouth;
> it shall not return to me empty,
> but it shall accomplish that which I purpose,
> and succeed in the thing for which I sent it.   (Isaiah 55.10–11)

Here is the conclusion of the prophecies of the great anonymous prophet of the exile, usually called Second Isaiah, in which he attempts to bring comfort to Israel by telling them that God is about to set them free to return to Jerusalem. The return has been foretold by the word of the Lord through the prophets and will now be accomplished by the power of that same word. The Persian emperor Cyrus, though he acts according to his own best intentions and without even being aware of the higher purpose of God, will be an instrument of that purpose.

The New Testament also testifies to the power of God's word in history. In Ephesians the 'sword of the Spirit, which is the word of God' (Ephesians 6.17) is to act against spiritual forces governing the world of human affairs. Likewise the book of Revelation pictures the 'sharp two-edged sword' coming from the mouth of 'one like a Son of Man' (Revelation 1.13, 16) and the sharp sword in the mouth of the one whose name is the Word of God to 'strike down the nations' (Revelation 19.13, 15).

And if God's word has powerful effects in the natural world and in history, it is equally powerful in the lives of individuals. In Hebrews:

> The word of God is living and active, sharper than any two-edged sword, piercing until it divides soul and spirit, joints from marrow; it is able to judge the thoughts and intentions of the heart.
>
> (Hebrews 4.12)

As we have already seen, both James and 1 Peter write of the word as a seed giving us new birth and carrying the power of salvation. Both apostles are taking their metaphor from Jesus' parable of the sower, in which 'the seed is the word of God' (Luke 8.11). Although the word has power in the lives of individuals, in this case, unlike those of the natural world or historical time, the outcome depends on personal response. Jesus makes it clear that although the seed has the power to grow, its fruitfulness will depend on the soil in which it is sown. We need to 'welcome' the word 'with meekness' before it can have its full effect (James 1.21).

The messengers

Both Old and New Testaments give an important role to human agents in the communication of God's word. It is the words the prophets are called to speak that will change both history and human hearts. In the case of reluctant Jeremiah:

> Then the LORD put out his hand and touched my mouth;
> and the LORD said to me,
> 'Now I have put my words in your mouth.
> See, today I appoint you over nations and over kingdoms,
>   to pluck up and to pull down,
>   to destroy and to overthrow,
>   to build and to plant.'   (Jeremiah 1.9–10)

Here is the word, both creative and destructive, working 'like fire' and 'like a hammer that breaks a rock in pieces' (Jeremiah 23.29) to change the course of history. Not only will Jeremiah foretell what will come to pass unless the leaders of his people change course, his words will actually bring those consequences about. In the same way, in Ezekiel's vision in the valley of dry bones (Ezekiel 37.1–11) it is the prophet's words that cause the bones to come together, put on flesh and live:

his words are to be the cause of the promised return from exile. It was the word of God in the mouths of the prophets that would bring about historical change, and in the New Testament the 'word of the Lord' that 'endures for ever' takes the form of 'the good news that was announced to you' (1 Peter 1.25), the gospel that contains the power to change the world.

Neither the prophet nor the evangelist is a mouthpiece, pure and simple; they are called not only to speak the word but also to embody it in their lives. Jeremiah was not a disinterested commentator on political events: part of his call was to shun both celebrations and public mourning and even to abstain from marriage as a sign of the times that were coming on Jerusalem (Jeremiah 16.1–9). Ezekiel was even to refrain from mourning when his wife died as a sign of the tragedy about to overwhelm the city (Ezekiel 24.15–24). And Paul could remind the church in Thessalonica of his 'labour and toil' and that of his fellow workers, of 'how pure, upright and blameless our conduct was towards you believers' (1 Thessalonians 2.9–10). To be entrusted with the powerful word of God was to be expected to live a life that reflected that word in the context in which it was to be spoken.

Yet the form of the word reflects the personality of the speaker. The poetry of Isaiah is very different from the priestly prose of Ezekiel, the elaborate and sometimes outlandish visions of Ezekiel different from the straightforward, insistent message of destruction given by Jeremiah. The powerful and triumphal poetry of Nahum, who revels in the destruction of Nineveh, is very different from that of the tender and emotional Hosea, hoping almost to the end for a stay of execution for Samaria. Yet each, with his own style and personality, was the bearer of the word of the Lord.

Word and Spirit

Towards the end of the Old Testament period there is a growing recognition of the link between the action of the word and the power of the Holy Spirit. From earliest times, it was assumed that the prophets, with their often strange behaviour, were guided by the unpredictable spirit of the Lord. At the time of the exile, Ezekiel criticizes the false prophets for following their own spirits (Ezekiel 13.3) though the implication – 'rather than the spirit of God' – remains implicit. But in the post-exilic passages of Isaiah there is an explicit parallel between word and Spirit:

Seek and read from the book of the LORD:
> not one of these shall be missing;
> none shall be without its mate.
For the mouth of the LORD has commanded,
> and his spirit has gathered them.   (Isaiah 34.16)

And as for me, this is my covenant with them, says the LORD: my
spirit that is upon you, and the words that I have put in your mouth,
shall not depart out of your mouth . . .   (Isaiah 59.21)

And these texts pave the way for the announcement:

The spirit of the LORD God is upon me,
> because the LORD has anointed me;
he has sent me to bring good news to the oppressed . . .
>   (Isaiah 61.1)

The New Testament is written in the light of the revelation of God
in the incarnate Word, Jesus Christ, and the gift of the Spirit to the
whole Christian community. Here too the Spirit of the Lord is linked
with the action of the word of God. In John's Gospel the new birth,
ascribed in 1 Peter to the word of the Lord, is said to be 'from the
Spirit' (John 3.8). In Luke and Acts, it is the gift of the Spirit that will
empower the apostles to be Jesus' witnesses (Luke 24.48–49; Acts 1.8).
Spirit and word go hand in hand in the proclamation of the gospel
and in building up the life of the Christian community so that it may
be a reflection and continuation of the life of Jesus himself.

In the mouths of the Old Testament prophets the word of God acts
as a powerful agent of change in the natural world and in historical time.
From Jesus' resurrection onwards Spirit and word act together to transform the community that bears his name and, with their cooperation,
transform the world. To reiterate, the goal of preaching is transformation: the preacher's commission is to set before the congregation the
'strange, new' world of the Bible, a vision of God's priorities and possibilities. And moreover, it is to preach for application. In the Bible,
hearing and obedience go together: to know God's will is to be expected
to do it. Its vision is for a community living under the rule of God
acting as 'salt' and 'light', influencing the world in both hidden and
obvious ways. 'The only hermeneutic of the gospel,' wrote Newbigin,
'is a congregation of men and women who believe it and live by it.'
The goal of preaching is the creation of congregations like this.

The preacher's authority

A sermon is a piece of spoken communication. It does more than simply convey information. It is an event with an outcome. The key question for the preacher is not so much, 'What do I want to say?' as 'What does God want to do?' Though the personality and style are her own, the preacher is seeking to convey a word of God for a specific situation, whose effect will be to encourage, enable, challenge or inspire so that the community more faithfully reflects in its own life the qualities of Christ.

What is the preacher's authority to do this? What gives her, with all her shortcomings, the right to undertake such a powerful commission? First, her authority comes from the Bible itself. The sermon will be located explicitly within the Christian tradition. Thus it will be true to Scripture. The Bible will supply a 'plausibility structure': a vision of a world transformed, whose values the community is called to live out in the present. The Bible is not simply the story of God's patient work with his people through the centuries; it is both the record of a process of reflection which has progressively moulded his people and an invitation to join that process and become part of that story. The preacher's authority comes from her commission to explain the world of Scripture and the character of the God revealed through it and to renew that invitation to join the community of God's people, for whom the story of the Bible is their story.

In a more particular way, the preacher's commission is in continuity with those of the prophets and Jesus himself, and shares some of the same characteristics. She is called to communicate God's word using the vehicle of human communication. The 'idiom' of the sermon, the personality through whom God's word is conveyed, will be her own. Just as Jesus, God's incarnate Word, lived as a man in a particular culture and historical period, so the preacher is a child of a particular time and place. Her task is to bear God's message for her own society, culture and congregation.

To do this the preacher must be subject to the word. We need to submit to the transforming effect of God's word and Spirit in our own lives. We may not be called upon to live out God's message in such extreme ways as Ezekiel or Jeremiah, but we cannot expect our lives to be unaffected by our calling. Preaching is persuasion: as preachers we are inviting our congregations into a closer relationship with God, a process that will inevitably change their lives, expose their sinful tendencies, refine their perception and reorder their priorities. If we are to do this effectively, our congregations must be able to see that we ourselves are submitting to this process. This does not mean that we need to be constantly telling people about ourselves in our sermons, but that our lives must be 'transparent': it must be apparent to any interested observer that what we preach we are prepared to practise.

Finally, the wisdom and power – by which the preacher discerns and conveys the word for the present moment and the community receives it and is changed by it – are those of the Holy Spirit. As preachers we need to welcome the work of God's Spirit in our lives and learn to discern the signs of the Spirit at work. There may be times when, like Timothy, we need to 'rekindle the gift of God' that is within us (2 Timothy 1.6). There may be occasions, perhaps regular retreats, when we need to take time out to listen to the 'sound of sheer silence' (1 Kings 19.12) in which God speaks. To be a preacher is to be open to the transforming effect of God's powerful word. This, perhaps above all, is the challenge of preaching.

Exercise 1F

If you are already a preacher, look back at your last half-dozen or so sermons. What would you say you were trying to *do* in each of those sermons? Or, to put it another way, what did you hope *God* would do as a result of it?

Exercise 1G

Consider the following question: Is Christian learning growing in understanding of Christian truth or learning to apply Christian truth to everyday situations?

Take 10 marks and allocate them between the two according to how important you think each to be. Reflect on the reasons that led you to your answer.

Exercise 1H

This exercise is an invitation to engage in a process of 'double listening': listening to God in the culture and in Christian tradition. Take one or more of the following areas and try to encapsulate the views either of society or of your local community and then of the Christian tradition:

- The purpose of daily work
- The right way to use money
- The way family relationships should work
- The role of sport in society
- The way we treat older people
- The role of sex in relationships
- The best uses of holiday times
- The responsibilities of people with political power.

Further reading

John L. Austin, 1975. *How to Do Things with Words*, 2nd edition. Cambridge, Massachusetts: Harvard University Press.

Rosalind Brown, 2009. *Can Words Express our Wonder?* Norwich: Canterbury Press, Chapter 4: 'The calling to preach'.

David Day, 2005. *Embodying the Word*. London: SPCK, Part 1: 'The word embodied in the preacher'.

David Day, 2005. 'The Lenten preacher', in David Day, Jeff Astley and Leslie J. Francis, eds, *A Reader on Preaching*. Farnham: Ashgate.

Shane Hipps, 2005. *The Hidden Power of Electronic Culture: How Media Shape Faith, the Gospel and the Church*. Grand Rapids, Michigan: Zondervan.

Marshall McLuhan, 1964. *Understanding Media*. London: Routledge and Kegan Paul.

Lesslie Newbigin, 1989. *The Gospel in a Pluralist Society*. London: SPCK, Chapter 18: 'The congregation as hermeneutic of the gospel'.

James R. Nieman, 2005. 'Preaching that drives people from church', in David Day, Jeff Astley and Leslie J. Francis, eds, *A Reader on Preaching*. Farnham: Ashgate.

John Stott, 1982. *I Believe in Preaching*. London: Hodder and Stoughton, Chapter 7: 'Sincerity and earnestness'; Chapter 8: 'Courage and humility'.

Paul Scott Wilson, 2004. *Preaching and Homiletic Theory*. Atlanta, Georgia: Chalice Press, Chapter 4: 'The eventful word'.

Stephen I. Wright, 2010. *Alive to the Word*. London: SCM Press, Chapter 5: 'The biblical grounding of preaching'; Chapter 6: 'Continuing the story: preaching in the ongoing purposes of God'.

2

The sermon as learning event

To change is to learn. A process of transformation is therefore a process of learning. In the previous chapter I suggested that the goal of preaching is transformation. Transformation involves people taking in new information, coming to see the world in a different way and ultimately changing their attitudes and behaviour. All these involve learning of one kind or another.

In order to teach effectively you need to know about the way people learn. In order to preach effectively, you need to know about the way people listen. If you hope to see a change in people's attitudes and behaviour, you need to know the way that attitude and behaviour change take place.

So before offering specific step-by-step advice on sermon preparation, this chapter looks at the way people learn, in the confident belief that if you, the reader, know how learning takes place, you will not only see the sense in the advice that follows but be equipped to use it both flexibly and intelligently. We will begin by looking at two vital components of learning: listening and remembering. As we shall discover, neither of these is a straightforward process. But both provide clues to the way our minds work, the way we take in, store and use information: in other words, the way we learn.

Listening

Before reading further, spend some time reflecting on the following questions:

- Are people natural learners? Do they seek God on their own account or do they need carrots and sticks to encourage them to learn?
- Do people come to learning with a 'blank slate' or do they bring existing knowledge and experience?

- Is the way that the Holy Spirit works in people's lives separate from and different from the way they ordinarily learn or does the Spirit work in and through the normal processes of learning?

We all come to the task of preaching with assumptions about the way people listen and learn. Many of these will have been derived from our own experience. Others will be conclusions drawn from observation and reflection. The questions above are designed to help you become aware of at least some of these. The answers you give to these questions will make all the difference to the way that you preach.

For example, if you believe that the members of your congregation are keen to learn and ready to change, then the topics you choose to preach about, the way you introduce them, your tone of voice and the way you phrase the sermon will all be different from what they will be if you believe that your congregation are resistant to learning and change. In practice, you probably decided that the answer lies somewhere between the two. People are open to varying degrees. Like the people in Jesus' parable of the sower, some have issues in their lives that interfere with their response to the word while others present 'good soil' for the gospel. In which case, another question occurs: how can I as preacher and pastor help to create favourable conditions for people to receive the word?

Many preachers assume that people's minds are, in effect, a 'blank slate' and that all we need to do to teach something is to pass over the information, making it as interesting and entertaining as possible. As we shall discover, however, this is most definitely a wrong assumption. Whatever the topic, people bring a great deal of prior experience, usually expressed in opinions, beliefs and sometimes deep-seated attitudes. Simply 'handing over' the new information will rarely be sufficient. We need to know how to engage with people's existing experience to give them the best chance of understanding and taking on board the new ideas and information we want to convey.

And finally, what is the role of the Holy Spirit? Does the Spirit use some separate channel, different from the way people normally learn, or does he work in and through the normal processes of learning? I myself am firmly of the opinion that, although the Holy Spirit is perfectly capable of doing extraordinary things and frequently does so, his usual mode of working is through the normal processes God has created. I have argued for this in an earlier book based on extensive research and have been pleased to see this position accepted in more and more Christian literature in the past few years.

The material of this chapter should help you to reflect further on each of these questions and more, and you may want to return to them for some further consideration at a later stage.

Encountering new information

How do you read a Sunday newspaper? Clearly there will be variation between different people, depending on our interests and the amount of time available. But allowing for these, there are likely to be some important similarities.

First, most of us will discard the portions of the paper we don't want because we are not particularly interested; for some the financial section, for others media, education, properties or sport. Then we begin with the section we enjoy most, are most interested in or judge most important. If this is the news section, you may begin with the front page then move through the paper scanning the headlines, picking out the articles of most interest. An intriguing headline may attract you to read an article about something new and unfamiliar; or you may be drawn to something about which you have a personal interest. With some articles you may read the first few paragraphs to get the gist of the story then skip through the rest to pick out the main points. With others, you will stick close to the text.

When you come to the opinion section, you may become even choosier. First you may well skip the columnists who you judge on past experience have nothing interesting to say. You will be guarded with those with whom you tend to disagree, choosing to read the article if it is about an area that is important to you but otherwise avoiding it and looking instead for the contributor you most enjoy or whose views you tend to agree with. On the other hand you may welcome the opportunity to engage with an opposing point of view. In general it is the writers we like and respect whose views we are most willing to consider, even if we disagree.

Our experience of reading a newspaper gives us a few simple pointers to the way people take in information. First and most important of all, listening is an active process. We do not passively absorb new information: we choose to engage with it. We are in an age of information overload. It is impossible to pay attention to all the information on offer at any given moment, so we grow used to deciding what is valuable and important, filtering out what we want and discarding the rest. Our decision to pay attention may be influenced by others: we may read the stories on the front page on the basis that the editor of the paper we have chosen has picked these out as most important. But beyond this we tend to exercise our own judgement as to the areas of life we consider interesting and important.

For the preacher the lesson is immediately apparent: we need in the first minute or two to give our hearers a reason to go on listening, some indication of what the sermon is going to be about and why it is going to be worth their while making the effort to pay attention. This is especially so in an age when people are used to multimedia communication involving a rapid succession of images and informal rather than formal language. The sermon will need to connect quickly with a question people may be asking or an issue that is important for them. As their minister, or as guest preacher on a special occasion, we stand in a similar position to the editor of the newspaper: many will be willing to allow us to choose a topic we think is important. But if we are to engage their attention, we need to show why it is relevant and important to them as well as ourselves.

Second, if the topic of the sermon is relevant and interesting this means that the hearers have experience of their own. More important, they will have an existing opinion about it. The preacher cannot assume that the minds of his audience are a blank slate, waiting to be told what to think. You need to respect the fact that your congregation already have some knowledge of the topic, or of topics closely related to it. You need the tacit permission of the congregation to share an opinion, even when this is God's opinion, clearly taught in Scripture. Yet all is not lost: as we shall see, there are ways of 'asking' for this permission and equally ways of helping the hearers to become aware of their own prior understanding and willing to change their minds.

Finally, the willingness of the congregation to listen depends on the trust and respect they have for the preacher. This is why the preacher's integrity of life and her relationship with the congregation is so vital. The primary message is the preacher's life: the more it is evidently faithful and demonstrates love for God and neighbour, the greater the respect with which her words will be received. And such respect is vital if we want to be in a position to disturb or challenge.

Having used the newspaper as an example of everyday 'listening', we will now examine the process in more detail. What are the barriers to listening and learning? If we recognize these we will be in a better position to help people engage.

Barriers to listening

Over some of the obstacles to listening the preacher has little or no control. One person may occupy his habitual seat near the back, despite the fact that he is growing deaf and has difficulty hearing. Another may come preoccupied by a difficult family or work situation. In the case of a third, a chance remark at the beginning of the sermon sends her off on a chain of thought that distracts her from the message. But some barriers are entirely within the preacher's control.

The first reason many people fail to listen, as we have seen, is that they are not interested in the topic. In this age of information overload, people are in the habit of sampling information to see if it is relevant and interesting. Unless the preacher can give them a good reason for listening in the first minute or two, they are likely to switch off. One of the most important functions of an introduction is to give a clear indication of what the theme of the sermon is going to be and the difference it could make to the listener. It can also be useful to give an indication of how the sermon is going to develop: to have a sense of the 'route' enables the listener actively to follow the preacher as she develops her theme and helps him to be ready for the conclusion when it arrives.

The second barrier to listening is often created by the preacher, who makes the sermon too difficult to understand. To be able to take in new information, we need enough existing knowledge to be able to make sense of it. I have a vivid memory of a conversation, when I was a curate, with one of our churchwardens, who was a nuclear physicist. He was the kind of person who was fascinated by the way things work and for whom no problem was too trivial to attempt a solution. On one occasion I met him in the church vestry just after he had solved the problem of the church boiler and set it working. Enthusiastically, he set out to tell me what had gone wrong and how he had been able to fix it. I was completely baffled. I did not have enough prior knowledge about boilers and their ways even to begin to comprehend what he was talking about.

It is easy for the preacher to do the same to her congregation. She has far more extensive background knowledge of the Bible than most, if not all, of them. She may fail to recognize those aspects of the passage that cause difficulty for most ordinary people – why Jesus told us to 'hate' our nearest relations, what Paul means by 'justi-fication' – because they are clear to her. In her reading of the com-mentary she may have gleaned a good deal of fascinating background information that she considers essential to a full understanding of the passage – even though it means nothing to her listeners because they do not know enough of the context to understand it. The issues in the passage she chooses to preach on may be those that are most important for biblical scholars rather than the hairdresser, the office worker and the grandmother in the back row.

To avoid this barrier you need to listen to your congregation so as to learn how they relate to the Bible and how much background knowledge you can take for granted. When considering the passage for the sermon, you will need to listen to it as far as possible with the ears of the congregation. You will need to be in a position to discern the issues in the passage nearest to their concerns. Where is the challenge in the passage? And is it the same for you as for your congregation? You will also need to recognize those aspects of the passage that are ripe for misunderstanding and be ready with a clear explanation.

It is also a great help to be aware of which character in the passage you most readily identify with: in the parable of the Pharisee and the tax-collector, for example, is it the tax-collector, the Pharisee, Jesus or the crowd listening to the story? In a complex passage from Romans, is it Paul or the church? In a small piece of research, Mark Powell discovered that most ministers tended to identify with Jesus in a Gospel story while most members of their congregations identified with the disciples. Clergy almost never identified with people con-demned in a passage, such as the Pharisees in the Gospels or the unfaithful Israelite kings of the Old Testament, whereas lay people frequently did (2007, pp. 59–60). So whose angle will you use in explaining the passage: one dominant point of view or a mixture of several? And how will you let your congregation know what you are doing and invite them to think along with you?

The third barrier to listening is not so much to do with under-standing as with emotion. Those existing opinions about the theme you have chosen, based on prior experience, may be reinforced with a great deal of emotional commitment. These can be the boulders in the soil that are hard to remove or the thorns and thistles that choke the word before it has a chance to grow. This is one reason why it can be extremely difficult to include anything about a current political issue into our sermons. For many people politics functions as an alternative commitment, separate from their commitment to Christ. Of course, it needs to come under his lordship, but showing people the need for this and helping them to respond is something that needs to be handled with wisdom and care. And politics is by no means the only subject on which people have strongly defended views: money and family relationships are just two others.

For some people those emotional commitments stray into the area of sinful attitudes. I once knew someone with a particularly critical tongue, which she used freely to control many of the other members of the church. Despite the fact that behaviour like this is condemned in the Bible, she seemed unable to see that what she was doing was wrong. My guess is that her habit of critical speech had grown out of deep unhappiness and insecurity. She was protecting herself against the impact of her past experience while in the process passing on to others the deep sense of unworthiness she felt. So it is with many of the sins that blight our lives and those of the people around us, and prevent us from growing closer to God and being secure in a sense of his love. The sermon is not a good vehicle for addressing situations like this. But if week by week the preaching is helping to reinforce an atmosphere of grace and acceptance, with the expectation of transformation, it may help to create a background against which they may be dealt with pastorally.

Finally, there is the habit of mind in which sermons are routinely ignored because they are not seen as relevant to life. One reason may be past experience: the person who at one stage in the past genuinely looked to the sermon for guidance and help with the problems encountered at work or in relationships, only to go away disappointed time after time. Another may be the continuing sacred–secular divide in people's thinking: the assumption that everything said in church has to do with a 'religious' domain of experience completely separate from everyday life.

Then there is the worldliness that fails to recognize the sermon as requiring a response. Eugene Peterson (2002) tells the story of the 'high-energy executive' who says to him after a service, 'This was wonderful, pastor, but now we have to get back to the real world, don't we?' 'I had thought we were in the most-real world,' Peterson comments, 'the world revealed as God's, a world believed to be invaded by God's grace and turning on the pivot of Christ's crucifixion and resurrection.' For people like the executive, worship is marginal to the 'real' business of making money. Christian commitment is a brand preference. The title of the essay is, 'The subversive pastor'. Peterson points out that Jesus had a technique for the spiritually hard-of-hearing: the parable, a story that drew people in further than they expected and left them with a choice to make. By subverting their rock-solid, unconsidered assumptions, he enabled them, if only momentarily, to see another view and gave them the possibility of change.

It may be discouraging to realize that there are so many potential barriers to listening, so it is important to remember that these barriers are not insuperable. As the research mentioned in Chapter 1 suggests, most people come to church with the definite intention of listening to the sermon and the desire to learn from it. And in the next chapter, as we dissect the process of sermon preparation, we will be addressing at several points the question of how to help people listen well.

Exercise 2A

Which of the following do you find most valuable in helping you to listen well to a sermon?

- When you respect the preacher and expect the sermon to be good?
- When the subject of the sermon is important to you?
- When you are able to identify with the way the preacher describes a life situation?
- When the sermon evokes appropriate feelings about the life situation described?
- When new information is clearly explained in a way you can understand?
- When the sermon has a clear sense of progression?
- When the preacher uses humour appropriately?
- Others . . .

Which of the following do you find a barrier to listening?

- When you have no interest in the topic?
- When the preacher fails to grab your attention at the beginning?
- When the preacher introduces a new section of the sermon without linking it to what has gone before?
- When there is no indication of what the outcome of the sermon ought to be?
- When the sermon challenges you to change in a way that is unwelcome?
- Others . . .

Further reading

Mary Mulligan and Ronald J. Allen, 2005. *Make the Word Come Alive: Lessons from Laity*. Atlanta, Georgia: Chalice Press.

Mary Mulligan et al., 2005. *Believing in Preaching: What Listeners Hear in Sermons*. Atlanta, Georgia: Chalice Press.

Eugene Peterson, 2002. 'The subversive pastor', in *Life at its Best*. Grand Rapids, Michigan: Zondervan.

Mark Allen Powell, 2007. *What Do They Hear? Bridging the Gap Between Pulpit and Pew*. Nashville, Tennessee: Abingdon Press.

Leonora Tubbs Tisdale, 1997. *Preaching as Local Theology and Folk Art*. Minneapolis, Minnesota: Fortress Press.

Remembering

Since both listening and memory are elements in the way our minds work to take in, store and use information, remembering shares many characteristics with listening. Like listening, it is an active process, deeply affected by our values and emotions. A look at memory, then, takes us deeper into our investigation of the way learning takes place. In particular, the way memory works highlights one crucial aspect of the way we listen and learn: the role of *interpretation*.

Mental models

If listening is an active process requiring effort and commitment, so is remembering. John Henry Newman expressed it like this in *The Idea of a University*:

> The enlargement [of the mind] consists not merely in the passive reception into the mind of a number of ideas hitherto unknown to it, but in the mind's energetic and simultaneous action upon and towards and among those new ideas . . . it is a making the objects of our knowledge subjectively our own, or . . . it is a digestion of what we receive, into the substance of our previous state of thought. It is an acquired illumination, a personal possession, and an inward endowment.
>
> (1858, p. 118)

In the last few pages I have mentioned existing understanding and opinions as predisposing people to listen in one way or another. Now here is Newman writing about 'the substance of our previous state of thought'. What he points to is the existence of 'mental models' through which we understand and, more importantly, interpret the world. A mental model brings together all past experience of a particular area into an internal 'picture' or way of understanding it. Thus a person's mental model of the Church is based on all his previous experience of Church and churches: the worship at his own local church and the different forms of worship he may have encountered when visiting others; his reading about the Church in newspapers, books and magazines, from clerical sex scandals through statistics of growth or decline to the pronouncements of archbishops; TV series about country or seaside vicars; experience of PCCs, day conferences, church days out and vicarage garden parties.

This mental model of 'Church' consists of what Jeff Astley (2002) calls an 'ordinary theology'. By this he points to the obvious fact that people without a formal theological training, who make up the overwhelming majority of Christians, nevertheless have an understanding of God and Christian faith. The 'lay person's' 'ordinary' theology of the Church is learned through experience and constantly developing. But rather than giving weight to those elements that academic theologians deem important for our understanding of the Church, 'ordinary theology' gives weight to whatever is significant and meaningful to the person who holds it.

Like any mental model, this 'theology' of Church will be a stereotype. Because there is too much information available, too much experience to make sense of, our mental models impose a structure on experience that simplifies in order to comprehend. In the case of the Church, one person may understand it principally as an institution, another as a group of caring people, a third as chiefly to do with worship and services.

Herein lies a warning to most of us who preach. Our mental model of the Church is not an 'ordinary', lay person's theology but a trained, academic theology. Just as an interior decorator will be aware of far more features in a room than someone without her interest and training, or a professional musician 'hear' more of a concert than an amateur enthusiast, so the theologically trained preacher will understand the Church and everything connected with it in a different way from her hearers. Without discarding our formal theological training we need to find ways of 'bridging the gap' in order to communicate in ways that people can understand.

This is all the more important because mental models are far more than passive structures of understanding. They also form a readiness to respond to a given area of experience. My mental model of the Church does not simply give me information about the Church; it also tells me how to interpret any new experience of church I may have. And it predisposes the way that I listen to any sermon about the Church. It enables me to respond, in Newman's words, 'energetically' and 'simultaneously' to new ideas, to 'digest them' and 'make them my own'.

This feature of mental models has a profound effect on the processes of memory. Because our mental models are telling us how to interpret experience, we tend to do just that: we interpret each new experience to fit in with what we expect. This was demonstrated by some striking experiments carried out by Sir Frederic Bartlett as long ago as the 1920s. In one he showed people a picture of a notice board next to a gate and then asked them to describe what they could remember. Even though the 'writing' on the notice board was deliberately left indistinct, most claimed to have been able to read 'Trespassers will be prosecuted'. In another experiment he showed 20 people a pattern of lines with the words 'an airoplaxe'. Nineteen of them remembered the words as 'an aeroplane'; the one who did not had not seen the lines as representing anything in particular. Bartlett's conclusion was that memory is essentially reconstructive: what we remember is what we think 'must have been' the case.

A further complication arises from an aspect of mental models that we have already seen in action: many of our beliefs are emotionally supported. John Hull makes this observation:

> The emotional value which is placed upon a construct must not be thought of as a mere feeling which is so to speak painted on the surface of an idea and which remains the same whatever colour it has . . . If I disapprove of fox hunting, I will place the construct in a constellation together with bull fighting, bear baiting, gladiatorial contests and other forms of inflicting cruelty for entertainment. If I approve of fox hunting, I will associate it with healthy outdoor life, the love of the countryside, the old English traditional values and so on . . . The fox hunting of which somebody approves is actually known in quite different a manner from the fox hunting of which somebody else disapproves. (1985, p. 106)

In other words, we have to reckon with a large amount of emotional commitment not just 'painted on the surface' of what we know but part and parcel of the way we structure and hold that knowledge. The person whose experience of church is of welcome, nurture, inspiring worship and close friendship 'knows' the church differently from the person alienated from church either by prejudice or personal experience.

Most people have deep convictions that they would prefer not be shaken, and this is especially so when it comes to matters of faith. We have already seen this to be an obstacle to listening, a reason why, in some cases, people may fail to 'hear' the preacher. In other cases, what the preacher says may be both heard and remembered, but remembered 'wrong', in a way that fits in with previous understanding, and particularly previous conviction. Getting to know our congregation may help us to anticipate some of the ways in which a particular point might be misunderstood and so help us to explain it clearly.

Preaching for remembering

What we remember, then, is what we are able to 'digest'. This means that its digested form may well be very different from the original. But just because someone may not be able to recount a sermon in any detail does not mean that they have remembered nothing. The measure of what is remembered is the way a person's mental models have changed as a result of what has been heard: the way she thinks and feels about a situation and responds to it the next time it is encountered. If a person deals differently with a challenging situation at work, begins to treat people more kindly or to pray in a more focused way, she has 'remembered' the sermon in which she heard about these things, even though she may not be able to recall a word of what was said.

In the next chapter we will look in detail at some of the ways of structuring a sermon so as to work with the mental models of the listener rather than against them. Here I will make a few general points. First, it is a perfectly proper aim on some occasions, perhaps many, to confirm and reassure the congregation in their faith. As Fred Craddock points out, the sermon may speak not only *to* but also *for* the congregation.

> If a minister takes seriously the role of the listeners in preaching, there will be sermons expressing for the whole church, and with God as the primary audience, the faith, the doubt, the fear, the anger, the love, the joy, the gratitude that is in all of us. The listeners say, 'Yes, that is my message; that is what I have wanted to say.'   (1985, pp. 26–7)

In a sermon like this, the preacher is not setting out to teach something new but to reinforce the old and familiar. There are many occasions and seasons in the life of a church when encouragement is called for and this will be the primary intention of such a sermon.

Such encouragement and reminder can strengthen existing belief in a culture increasingly hostile to Christian faith and also help to build community by reinforcing a sense of shared commitment.

Second, the preacher can structure the sermon in such a way as to affirm an existing belief before moving on to its corollary. This is something we frequently see Jesus doing. The beauty and profusion of nature teaches us that God cares for his creation – so will he not care much more for us? God forgives each one of us freely – so ought we not to forgive one another? In the same way, a sermon on giving, which is clearly a challenging subject for most people, might begin by affirming God's generosity and giving examples of the positive effects of human generosity before suggesting that God looks for the same generosity from us.

A variation of this is to begin with some examples, stories or sayings with which members of the congregation are likely to identify. I once began a sermon on the mystery of suffering by quoting the words of a man I had once met on a hospital visit expressing his bewilderment and loss of faith on the loss of his son, who had died in an accident on his twenty-first birthday. I then told the story of a young mother only recently confirmed who had lost a baby but whose faith had been strengthened through the support she had received from Christian friends. I summed up these stories by describing the different ways in which people respond to suffering, including those who say, 'I don't understand what has happened, but I am going to go on trusting God.' One relative newcomer to the church so strongly identified with all three of these stories or quotations that her faith was immeasurably strengthened and she became a regular member.

A further variation is to begin not so much with a story or quotation with which people are likely to identify as with a question that may be on their minds. The question may emerge from the passage: why, in Matthew's version of the parable of the great feast, is the master, who seems to represent God, so hard not only on his enemies but on the guest without a wedding garment (Matthew 22.1–14), or what point is Jesus really trying to make in the parable of the dishonest manager (Luke 16.1–9)? But by far the most effective questions are those that arise from daily life and current events, the questions that people are actually asking and that have significance for them. If we know what these are, and are able to describe and explore them in our sermons, in particular if we are able to empathize with the feelings that arise for people coping with difficult and problem situations, there is a far greater chance of congregations both listening and remembering well.

Exercise 2B

Think about the sermons you picked out for Exercise 1A. What features of these sermons do you think made them memorable?

- The sermon helped me with something I had been confused about or was wrestling with.
- The sermon confirmed a belief that was important to me.
- The sermon challenged me and made me rethink what I had always believed.
- The preacher used a particularly vivid illustration.
- The sermon included a memorable sound-bite.
- The preacher gave a particularly clear explanation of a complex issue.
- The preacher suggested a way I was able to put the sermon into practice.
- Others . . .

References

Fred Craddock, 1985. *Preaching*. Nashville, Tennessee: Abingdon Press.
John Henry Newman, 1858. *The Idea of a University*. London: Longmans, Green.

Further reading

Jeff Astley, 2002. *Ordinary Theology*. Farnham: Ashgate.
David Heywood, 2004. *Divine Revelation and Human Learning: A Christian Theory of Knowledge*. Farnham: Ashgate.
John Hull, 1985. *What Prevents Christian Adults from Learning?* London: SCM Press.

Learning

We have looked at two of the specific 'components' of the learning process, listening and remembering. We have seen that listening is an active process; it requires a decision to pay attention to some new information or situation, whether conveyed by the written or the spoken word. Because listening is an active process, we have seen that it is also selective: congregations need to make a decision to 'make room' for the preacher's message before they will hear anything at all. There are a number of barriers that prevent people from listening well. If the message is too complex they may not understand. Perhaps most powerful are the emotional barriers that make people reluctant to hear a particular message. Listening to a sermon begins with a decision to trust the preacher and a disposition to value what he or she has to say.

Then we saw that memory depends on our previously existing mental models. These may have powerful emotional components; in fact, it is from the prior expectations set up by our mental models that the emotional barriers to listening may come. To incorporate a message in our memory means changing our mental models: 'digesting' what we receive 'into the substance of our previous state of thought'. It is therefore important for the preacher to understand the congregation's 'ordinary theology' and to provide the 'space' for the 'energetic' working required to incorporate the preacher's message into their own understanding. This is a process that requires energy, even when it is mainly subconscious, but the outcome is learning. It is time, then, to bring together these observations about listening and remembering in an overall look at learning.

To focus on the potential difficulties of listening and remembering may be discouraging. So it is important to remember that learning does, in fact, take place all the time and may include whole new areas of knowledge and experience. The parents of a new baby have a lot to learn in order to care for it and bring it up, but almost all learn this reasonably successfully. Anyone beginning a new job must rapidly learn the ropes, but it is perfectly possible to be well on the way to mastering the requirements by the end of the probationary period. Similarly, research suggests that most regular churchgoers are well disposed towards the sermon and willing to listen. Our task, then, is to reward that attention with sermons that genuinely help them to learn and grow in their faith.

The learning cycle

If preaching is to make the most effective contribution to this process of learning and change, it is important that it goes 'with the grain' of the way people learn. In fact, if there is one major reason why preaching is less effective than it could be, I would say it is the neglect of this basic principle. The primary question for the preacher is not, 'What do I want to say?' but, 'What do I want people to hear, remember

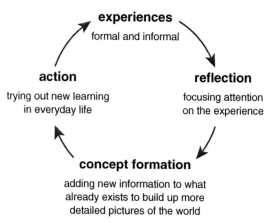

Figure 2.1

and learn?' Only when we know how people learn are we in a position to decide what to say and how to say it.

Since the 1980s the 'learning cycle' formulated by David Kolb has become familiar to educators everywhere as a rough and ready way of describing the steps through which people pass on the way to learning. The learning cycle has four phases (see Figure 2.1).

Experiences sum up the many and varied situations which might give rise to learning: reading the daily paper, chatting with a neighbour, encountering a problem at work, having an accident, attending an in-service training day, listening to a sermon.

Some of these are what we might call 'formal' learning situations: in other words, they are deliberately created with the purpose of helping people to learn. But formal learning situations themselves vary greatly. As well as planned and structured events like a day course or Bible study group, they include reading the newspaper or following the instructions for a recipe or putting up a shelf. The informal events through which learning may take place are even more varied: an argument with a spouse, illness or bereavement, moving house, a casual conversation – all these may become the source of significant new learning. In fact, human beings are learning all the time, sometimes very quickly. We learn in order to orientate ourselves to our surroundings, to cope with the multiple demands of life, to maintain good relationships with colleagues and loved ones, or simply out of curiosity and fascination.

Of course, there are many experiences that we don't learn from. Experiences come and go so quickly that it is impossible to pay attention to everything that happens to us; just as in reading the newspaper, we naturally select what we judge most important. Some experiences leave us 'baffled', uncertain how to make sense of them. And in some cases we protect ourselves from possible pain by thinking about them as little as possible. The goal of the preacher, then, is to make the sermon as welcome and accessible as possible as a potential learning event.

Likewise, *reflection* embraces a range of activities through which we analyse or mull over the experience, making connections and looking for ways of understanding it; these too may be formal or informal, from writing out an accident report or recording the results of a scientific experiment to quietly thinking or talking over an experience with a friend. In reflection we are making connections between the new experience, whether formal or informal, and our existing mental models. We are beginning to make sense of it in terms of what we already know, to incorporate it into our existing way of seeing the world, while at the same time looking out for the unexplained, seeking to respond to those parts of the experience that challenge our existing understanding.

The reflection process may be short or long. It may take us by surprise with its lightning quickness, confronting us with new insights almost unbidden. Or it may take much longer: in some cases months or even years. This is why time for reflection is so often a valuable part of the learning process. The connections called forth in reflection will depend on those parts of our existing mental models that 'resonate' with the new experience. Often, these are emotional as well as conceptual. The most powerful will be those that seem most important to us. At the heart of reflection is often the question, 'What do I think is "really" happening here?' If I am reflecting on an argument, was I in the wrong, or was it my colleague or partner? Or perhaps we are both wrong? In the case of a training day, what do I most need to take away from this? What will the boss expect? What will colleagues expect? What do I find most interesting? What will help me get on? And in the case of a sermon on family life, how is this relevant to me? Will it help me relate better to my son? Is it challenging me about the way I treat my parents? Does the preacher's experience ring true to mine? What is the source of his authority?

At the stage of *concept formation* we come to a conclusion. To echo the quotation from Newman, we 'make the objects of knowledge subjectively our own', incorporate or 'digest' them into 'the substance of our previous state of thought'. The outcome may be trivial or far-reaching. We may simply incorporate the experience as new knowledge into our existing mental model. On the other hand, the new insight may lead to a whole new way of seeing so that our mental model changes, perhaps radically.

Since an emotional dimension is integral to our mental models the outcome may be a change of attitude or the adoption of a new set of values. On the other hand, something as far-reaching as this requires considerable adjustment and therefore a great deal of energy. Since so much of Christian faith addresses precisely these areas, challenging us about our attitudes and values, learning to live as a Christian requires considerable time for reflection and a great deal of community support. Sermons may contribute to the kind of change required, but cannot achieve it on their own. As we will see, the Church's ministry of preaching needs to be part of a 'balanced diet' of all-round learning.

Finally, learning is not complete without the *action* phase of the cycle. The new insight or attitude must be put into practice and lived out. In some formal learning situations, the action response is built in. In science, for example, the conclusions drawn from one experiment or set of experiments lead naturally to the next experiment. Usually a training day results in changed practice. Often the same is true of less formal situations. If I conclude that the argument with my spouse was largely my fault I will approach the topic in a different way next time.

Often, however, the action phase of the cycle is less easy to define. The outcome of the learning may be a new insight or simply a different way of seeing a situation. It may be difficult to define exactly how the new insight is to be expressed in practice. Nevertheless, if learning has genuinely taken place, there will be some difference. All genuine learning leads to change. It is just that what we have learned is so bound up with our whole way of seeing the world that the difference it makes is difficult to tease out.

The action phase of the learning cycle leads to the next significant new experience. But the person's mental models are now different. In a Christian context, her 'ordinary theology' has changed. So the next 'new' experience may, in fact, be a familiar experience seen in a new way. Learning about the meaning of the Communion service, for example, may lead to someone experiencing the service in a whole new way, gaining more insights and continuing to learn. A training day on 'God in the workplace' ought to lead to someone approaching her daily work in a new way, reconsidering many of her habitual judgements and routines, learning to pray about her problems with a new expectancy, and through all these changes continuing to learn as the cycle repeats itself, perhaps on a daily basis.

EXERCISE 2C

Look back over the last few years and choose something you have learned which has been significant for you. It could be:

- new *information*, e.g. I learned about conservation methods used in the National Park;
- a new *skill*, e.g. I learned to play the guitar;
- a new *understanding* or *perspective*, e.g. I learned about the impact of the First World War on the role of women;
- a new *sensibility*, e.g. I learned to appreciate Picasso's paintings;
- a new *attitude*, e.g. I learned not to be prejudiced against people who speak a different language;
- a new *insight* into yourself, your relationships with other people or with God, e.g. I learned how I tend to dominate in certain situations.

Use the following questions to help you:

1 What did you learn? Can you describe it in one sentence?
2 What were the circumstances in which you learned? How far was it a planned educational event (e.g. a course or training day)? How far did it happen in the course of everyday life?
3 How far were the circumstances important in helping you to learn, or how far were they an obstacle?
4 What part did other people play in your learning? Did they consciously set out to teach you or was their part unplanned, perhaps without their realizing it?
5 How far were your relationships with other people important in helping you to learn, or how far were they an obstacle?
6 What part did you play in your learning? Did it require much effort or practice? Was it painful to learn a new insight?
7 What was it that motivated you to learn? What kept you going when it was difficult or painful?

Further reading

Anton Baumohl, 1984. *Making Adult Disciples*. London: Scripture Union.

Sylvia Downs, 2008. *Making Learning Happen*. London: Downs Publications.

Norma Cook Everist, 2002. *The Church as Learning Community*. Nashville, Tennessee: Abingdon Press.

Parker Palmer, 1983. *To Know as We are Known*. London: HarperCollins.

Jenny Rogers, 2007. *Adults Learning*, 5th edition. Buckingham: Open University Press.

Learning through reflection

At the start of this chapter I stated my conviction that the Holy Spirit works through the natural processes of learning: that the ways in which we learn about God and grow in Christian faith are the same as those by which we learn about everything else. We might want to say that the presence of the Spirit offers an added dimension to Christian learning, but this may be to make a false distinction between 'Christian' learning and every other kind of learning. God, through his Spirit, wants to be involved in every part of our lives, not just the ones we label 'Christian'. And since this is so, we can expect the Spirit to be involved in every part of our learning.

So where do we find God in the learning cycle? Some will point to the action and experience phases. According to this view, we encounter God when he does something in our lives or the life of our church; or when he speaks to us, either directly or through circumstances; or through our 'Christian' experiences, whether in worship or service. All this is true, but if God by his Spirit is genuinely to guide and inspire our learning we need to find him equally in the reflection and concept-formation phases. We need to invite or allow the Spirit to help us make the connections between our experience and our mental models, and to guide the conclusions we draw. In fact, we need to 'open up' our mental models to the presence of God's Spirit in our lives so that we learn gradually to see the world 'through God's eyes', to echo in our own lives the way God thinks and feels about the world.

This, in my eyes, is what Christian learning is all about: not simply learning *about* God and Christian faith, but learning to *see the world* through the lens of Christian faith and worship. The process through which we gradually grow in this ability has two aspects. One is learning to interpret our ordinary daily experience – the demands of the workplace, our relationships with colleagues and family, the life of society and the wider world – in the light of our understanding of God's nature and purposes for the world. The other is much more challenging: it involves allowing our experience to raise questions for us about what we believe, to reflect on experience in the light of Christian faith not simply in order to understand the experience from a Christian point of view but with a view to understanding our faith better.

The first involves refining our mental models through coming to understand areas of our lives in the light of our existing beliefs about God: perhaps through learning that forgiveness, when practised at work, can have the same kind of revolutionary effects as when practised in the church. The second may involve a significant change in our mental models, a new view of God and his purposes: we may come to learn that the worship God looks for does not depend on liturgical tradition or the lack of it, but comes from the heart and is expressed in action. In practice, although it is possible to distinguish between these two types of change, they often go together: we grow in our understanding of God and of his world at the same time.

These two aspects of reflection go on for most people a great deal of the time. People are always asking questions about God. The person who asks, 'If God is good and powerful, why is there so much suffering in the world?' is reflecting in this way, whether or not he considers himself a Christian. Many people find, on identifying themselves as Christians, that friends have a store of questions they want to ask and issues they want to reflect on. In some cases it can be regular churchgoers, people who have always thought of themselves as Christians, who are most incurious about God and his ways, or who think they already have all the answers sewn up.

But leaving aside this minority, reflection is by far the most important and far-reaching way in which people learn and grow in their faith. *And it is taking place all the time.* People are always encountering situations that force them to think and reflect, the unfamiliar and challenging, conflict situations, major decisions, tragedies, milestones, reflecting on these and drawing conclusions. Often, however, they reflect in an uninformed way: they find it difficult to make connections between the experience and their 'ordinary theology', their mental models of God and his ways. And sometimes, this means that they move on from the incident or situation baffled or uncertain, with less confidence about God's place in their lives and in the world than they had before.

To be able to reflect well, people first need guidance on the kinds of questions to be asking: questions like, 'Where is God in this situation?' 'What does God want me to learn through this?' 'What is God's call to me?' or simply, 'What would Jesus do?' Then they need confidence and permission to draw on the riches of Christian tradition: the Bible, worship and liturgy, hymns and poetry, stories of Christians past and present and, for those who can manage it, formal theology. This means that knowledge itself is useful as a storehouse or treasure chest for future reflection, as long as knowledge is not taken to be sufficient on its own. Then they need to recognize the attitudes that enable us to reflect well and those to avoid: openness to the unfamiliar rather than dismissiveness; patience to wait for insight rather than anxiety or hurry; willingness to change rather than fear. And, importantly, readiness to listen to others: no one reflects alone; we are all part of Christ's body and to reflect is to draw on the corporate wisdom of that body and of Christian tradition.

Thankfully, a variety of frameworks are now available to help people make reflection a part of their lives. Some of these are listed as further reading. Unfortunately, for many people 'theological reflection' has been surrounded by mystery and quickly dismissed. But my conviction is that when it is seen as an approach to the learning cycle in which we are open to the involvement of God's Holy Spirit, the element of mystery is soon dispelled. The proof of the pudding is in the eating, and more and more people are beginning to learn and grow through the approaches listed.

EXERCISE 2D

As an approach to reflective learning, try this example of 'critical incident analysis', based on the Grove booklet by Charles Chadwick and Phillip Tovey (2005):

1 Describing the incident

Choose a significant event and answer the following questions:

(a) When, approximately, did the event happen? (Give the month/year)
(b) Where would you put the event on the scale below?

1	2	3	4	5	6
(Good)				(Bad)	

(c) Describe what happened as fully as possible.

(d) What were your feelings at the time?

(e) What were your immediate reactions and judgements?

2 **Reflecting on the incident**

(a) Does the event remind you of anything in the Bible? (Either one or several passages may come to mind: try to take note of each one.)

(b) What do you think God might be telling you through this passage? (If more than one passage came to mind, choose one that seems likely to be fruitful.)

(c) What does the passage tell you about yourself?
  (i) About your strengths and weaknesses?
  (ii) About the values and assumptions which guide what you do?
  (iii) About what you know and do not know?

(d) What have you learned from this passage?

(e) What might you do differently next time?

(f) Returning to the incident, how do you see it now?

Further reading

Helen Cameron et al., 2012. *Theological Reflection for Human Flourishing.* London: SCM Press.

Charles Chadwick and Phillip Tovey, 2005. *Growing in Ministry Using Critical Incident Analysis*, 2nd edition, Grove P84. Cambridge: Grove.

Ian M. Fraser, 2005. *Reinventing Theology as the People's Work*, 4th edition. Glasgow: Wild Goose.

Laurie Green, 2009. *Let's Do Theology*, 2nd edition. Oxford: Mowbray.

Patricia O'Connell Killen and John de Beer, 1994. *The Art of Theological Reflection.* New York: Crossroad.

Roger Walton, 2009. *The Reflective Disciple.* Peterborough: Epworth.

Preaching for learning

If our ministry of preaching is to be effective we need to do at least two things: to understand the role of sermons in the context of the learning that is already taking place in our congregations through reflection; and to preach in such a way that our hearers have the best chance of listening, remembering, learning and putting the message into practice. The person who has merely listened to a sermon has not learned anything. Learning only occurs when he goes on to reflect on what he has heard, draw conclusions and put them into practice.

So what role does preaching play? Like health foods, sermons work best as part of a 'balanced diet'. The promotion of both individual and corporate transformation requires at least two other vital components: effective pastoral care and a process of continuing reflection on the church's shared life. Many of the changes required by Christian discipleship are far-reaching, requiring changes of attitudes and values. This kind of change usually requires the support of a loving and trustworthy community, a climate of openness to one another, trust and practical care. Without a community capable of nurturing and supporting such change, preaching for transformation is likely to be limited in its fruitfulness. As well as trust and care, the community also needs to encourage a habit of reflection. This means that reflection will be a regular part of the congregation's corporate life, supported by attitudes such as the desire to be faithful to God's calling and the willingness to face the cost of change and growth.

Many of the events and experiences capable of leading to deeper knowledge and faith in God arise from pastoral crises or times of pressure such as the illness of a family member, conflict or redundancy at work. At such times the person who comes alongside to provide care and support may also be able to raise questions like, 'Where is God in these events?' and 'How do you think he is calling you to respond?' Where God's people are equipped with the tools of theological reflection and the confidence that God is indeed to be found even in the worst of times, such situations may become opportunities for growth and change. Regular study groups may also play their part, especially if the discussion is allowed to move on from interpretation of the biblical text to its application in everyday life, space is created for the discussion of relational and work-based issues, doubts and problems, and an expectation is created of mutual support and prayer together.

The more that qualities like grace and mercy, love, goodness and self-control, willingness to accept rebuke lovingly given, to forgive and be forgiven are evident in the life of the church, the more effective it will be in promoting transformation. Attitudes are learned in relationships, 'caught' rather than 'taught'. Where the qualities of Christian life are evident as a normal pattern, and the culture of the whole church encourages honest reflection and the expectation of change, people are more likely to accept the pattern they experience in the church as appropriate for themselves.

'The primary shift in a learning congregation,' writes Thomas Hawkins, 'is from using people to create a better congregation to using the congregation to nurture better people. Experiences in ministry become occasions for reflection and learning, for constructing a fresh vision of new life in Christ' (1997, p. 26). In a congregation committed to transformation, church councils, choirs, children's and young people's groups and teams of all kinds within the life of the church will meet to focus not only on the task at hand but also on its relation to the coming of God's kingdom and on the quality of their life together. Thus, alongside effective pastoral care, a transformational community requires effective leadership, capable of stimulating and guiding a process of reflection.

Without the balanced diet that includes effective pastoral care and leadership in reflection, preaching will not be particularly effective in helping to bring about transformation. But as an element in that balanced diet sermons have a vital contribution to make. First, they can help to nurture and sustain the climate of learning. Using examples from the Bible and the present day, drawing attention to the teaching of Jesus and the apostles, they can create and reinforce the assumption that the Christian life is one of gradual change. In some cases, as we noted earlier, creating such a climate may require the skilful use of parables, drawing in the reluctant and leaving them with an awkward question. But in most the congregation will be only too willing to follow where the preacher leads. Hawkins (p. 26) notes that in many cases a thinking climate is more sought after and promotes greater commitment than the attribute of a church often seen as of greatest importance, pastoral care.

The teaching function of the sermon also has a key part to play: the preacher will regularly and consistently present the pattern of Christian life. Many of the stories of the Gospels feature individuals encountering Jesus, often out of need, at other times in friendship, confrontation or bewilderment. Such stories can promote reflection on our own encounters with him and open up the possibility of new experiences. They also point to the characteristics of Jesus himself, his obedience to the Father, his indifference to status and personal comfort, his willingness to confront hypocrisy. Or the New Testament epistles offer teaching on how to relate to employers and employees, parents, children, spouses and fellow church members.

Most of the reflection taking place in a congregation will concern the problems of everyday life. This means it is important for sermons both to address these problems and to model some ways of reflecting on them. Tragically, this is an opportunity largely neglected in many congregations. A survey by the London Institute of Contemporary Christianity revealed that 50 per cent of those questioned could not remember hearing a sermon about daily work. Almost three-quarters said that their church helped them no more than a little with issues in the workplace and almost a quarter that their church provided no help at all. Even with the issues of home – parenting, coping with elderly parents, loneliness or finance – some 60 per cent rated the help they received from their church as inadequate (Greene and Cotterell, 2003).

Alongside the importance of a balanced diet is that of preparing sermons with one eye on the way people learn. This means keeping the phases of the learning cycle in mind. First and foremost, it is vital that the preacher understands her congregation's 'ordinary theology'. This is their 'starting point', their existing 'mental model'. Of course, there will often be very wide differences between the ways different people in the same congregation understand Christian faith. But prolonged and careful listening will often reveal some commonly held misconceptions, shared attitudes, frequently asked questions, areas where there is a shared hunger for greater understanding. Time spent listening to people talking about their faith is rarely wasted.

Next, as I have already written at some length, the sermon needs to connect with the life experience of the congregation. But third, it is important to create space for reflection. The key here, I think, is to remember that a good sermon is not so much a monologue as a dialogue. Even if you are the only one doing the talking, the sermon is a conversation. As you speak, the congregation are thinking, weighing what you are saying, asking themselves whether they agree, perhaps wondering how it might apply. It will help them immensely if you give them the opportunity to become aware of their existing mental models. A story about someone with whom they might identify is just one way of doing this. Another is a case study with a question: 'Do you think he was right?' or 'What would you have done?' Another is to ask the question, 'What do you think?'

The next phase of the cycle is concept formation. This lies at the heart of preaching. The preacher is seeking to introduce his congregation to a new way of seeing: to 'reframe' the congregation's experience, so as to enable them to see it through the lens of God's character and rule, to help them to become, in mind and heart, citizens of God's kingdom.

Thus, the aim of a sermon might be to reframe a particular situation in the church or family, workplace or national life. Even in the newspapers the banking crisis has led to the reframing of commercial life in terms of greed rather than prosperity. The Bible contains a wealth of resources with which to examine the world of commerce from a number of points of view and to pose the question of how God sees this sphere of activity. Similarly, a time of communal or racial tension offers the possibility of reflecting on the Old Testament's tradition of welcome for the stranger or Jesus' willingness to break down barriers of race and religion.

Congregational learning and change can also come about as a result of reframing the stories of the congregation's past. Almost all congregations preserve stories of its founders and heroes and the way these are told help to form the congregation's culture. The story of an organ built from second-hand parts by members of the congregation was a powerful symbol for one church. Its members had themselves been gathered from various parts of London on to a relatively new housing estate, and building their own organ had been an important element in the process of forming community. In another congregation, one very powerful story was of a lay leader whose life had been transformed overnight by a dramatic experience of the Holy Spirit, which had also involved a miraculous healing. But for this same church, two tragic deaths in quick succession had brought about a sense of bewilderment and a fear that God had abandoned them. This congregation desperately needed to be enabled to discover God's presence in the tragic events and to tell the story in a different way. In some cases, the church may need to be encouraged to find new stories, perhaps through reclaiming the neglected events of the past, of hope instead of despair, reconciliation in place of conflict, the excitement of new things in place of nostalgia for the 'good old days'.

Concept formation is not complete until it leads to action. The goal of preaching is transformation: not simply changed minds but changed lives. And research tells us that congregations want application: they want preaching that translates into real life. On the other hand, it is important to remember that the listener is the expert on the circumstances of his own life. He may be in a better position to see how the passage applies to him than you are. Should you want to present a definite application, there are ways of asking permission to do so. You can frankly say, 'This is how it seems to me.' You might share the specific challenge in the passage to you personally and ask listeners to consider whether they are challenged in the same way, or perhaps some other. You can signal your conclusion as something to be considered before you state it. You can tell a story that illustrates one way in which the message you want to give has been applied but go on to suggest that there might be other ways.

What all these have in common is that they are ways of giving the congregation 'space' for their own side of the conversation and their own conclusions, allowing them to make the message their own or helping them to be aware when they have chosen not to. In this way they work with the listener's existing mental model rather than against it. They also implicitly acknowledge the relationship you are seeking: not one of domination, not that of the expert with all the answers, but as a fellow disciple willing to make yourself vulnerable in the process of leading the congregation's thinking about life and faith.

Finally, remembering requires an effort: in Newman's words, an 'energetic and simultaneous action'. If you are to create a conversation, to give people space to reflect on what you are saying, it is important not to say too much. Your listeners need time to connect the new thing you want to share, the new insight you want them to think about, with the whole of their previous experience to see how it fits and the difference it might make. This is why it is so important that sermons have one simple aim. To say too much reduces the chances of a congregation engaging with and remembering anything of the sermon. One point, made and instantiated in a variety of ways, is usually more effective than several different points in quick succession.

But this takes us into sermon preparation, which is the subject of the next chapter.

Exercise 2E

To what extent do you think it is for the preacher to decide on the topic for the sermon week by week, based on his knowledge and understanding of the Christian faith, and to what extent do you think the preacher should be responsive to the questions and issues that arise from the congregation?

Allocate 10 marks between these two alternatives to get a sense of how you balance the two and then try to give a reason for your answer.

EXERCISE 2F

Below is a list of some of the characteristics of adults as learners, drawn from extensive research. Taking each attribute one at a time, describe the features of the sermon that will best help the typical adult listener.

Adults learn best:

- when their experience is respected;
- when they have the opportunity to connect new information with their existing experience;
- when they can see the direct personal relevance of any new information;
- when they are allowed to set their own goals.

EXERCISE 2G

Below are some further characteristics of adult learners. This time, taking the characteristics one by one, describe the 'balanced diet' of which preaching needs to be a part that will best help the typical adult to grow in her Christian life.

Adults learn best:

- when there is a variety of learning activities;
- when the learning environment is comfortable;
- in peer groups interacting freely;
- when they can evaluate themselves;
- when they can see progress for their efforts.

References

Mark Greene and Tracy Cotterell, 2003. *Imagine How We Can Reach the UK*. London: LICC.

Further reading

Margaret Cooling, 2005. *Creating a Learning Church*. Oxford: Bible Reading Fellowship.

Charles R. Foster, 1994. *Educating Congregations*. Nashville, Tennessee: Abingdon Press.

Thomas R. Hawkins, 1997. *The Learning Congregation*. Louisville, Kentucky: Westminster John Knox Press.

Joseph R. Myers, 2007. *Organic Community*. Grand Rapids, Michigan: Baker Books.

John H. Westerhoff III, 2012. *Will Our Children Have Faith?* 3rd edition. New York City: Morehouse.

3

A step-by-step guide to sermon preparation

If you want to bake a cake, you need to include certain basic ingredients. You can vary the amounts and there is a huge variety of other things you can add to make cakes of many different kinds. But without the basics, you don't have a cake. In a similar way every sermon requires a certain number of basic ingredients. You can mix these in different proportions and include a variety of other things but without the basics you won't have a sermon that communicates well. To list these basic ingredients is relatively easy. They are:

- a clear message
- a suitable structure
- faithful interpretation of Scripture
- appropriate application of the message
- visual imagery that allows the listeners to engage with their imaginations
- the language of speech
- clear signals at points of transition
- an introduction
- and a conclusion.

But listing the ingredients is the easy part. Knowing how to use them well takes years of practice. The aim of this chapter is to set out the basics of how to use each of these ingredients and combine it with the others. To become a preacher, however, requires the discipline of reflecting on our sermons, alone and with the help of others, reviewing each aspect of the sermon in order to improve.

In my own case, the work I did to prepare the course of workshops that forms the basis for this chapter highlighted some areas where I needed to improve. In particular, I realized that my preaching had got into a rut: over the previous few years I had used almost exclusively one type of sermon structure. Writing this chapter has highlighted another area requiring attention: the use of 'handles' or signals at points of transition in the sermon. Learning to preach is a life-long process, but this is a reflection of the responsibility we bear as ministers of God's word.

So let us look at the ingredients of the sermon one by one.

Getting the message

The three stages of the sermon

The creation of a sermon has three phases:

1 deciding on the message for the sermon;
2 preparing the sermon;
3 preaching the sermon.

Sometimes these three stages get mixed up. For example, occasionally when preaching you may decide to put your notes to one side and preach unscripted. In other words, you will be doing your preparation at the same time as your preaching. While this is not always wrong, experience will soon tell you that it is easy to make a mistake when departing from your script, such as losing your thread or preaching for too long, so you need to be cautious about doing it.

In the same way and for the same reasons, it is important to distinguish between getting the message and preparing the sermon. Knowing your message is the heart of sermon preparation and all the other ingredients depend on it. Trying to do too much preparation before you have decided on your message is likely to lead to mistakes: you may be trying to say too much for one sermon, or you may be allowing a striking illustration to play the lead role rather than serving the sermon as a whole. Ideally, then, we should decide what our message is going to be at an early stage of preparation. Only when we know the message are we in a position to decide how to structure the sermon, the right illustrations to choose, how best to frame our introduction and conclusion, and so on.

Sometimes, however, this doesn't happen. Your message may only become clear at a late stage of preparation. When this happens it will be important to re-evaluate all the work you have done so far so as to make sure that the shape of your sermon really serves the message you have decided upon.

The 'message' of the sermon has three aspects:

The content: knowing what you want to say

What is the 'information content' of the sermon going to be? What do you want to remind people of, or teach them for the first time? If you aim at nothing, you are sure to hit it! And if you don't know what it is you really want to say you are likely to end up not saying very much that is of value.

The content of your message should be a true reflection of the message of the Bible passage on which you are preaching. Don't be tempted to use the passage as a peg on which to hang your own thoughts. Your congregation will not be built up or spiritually transformed by listening to your thoughts but through engaging with the word of God. It's vital to allow the passage to speak to you before you speak to the congregation. And it needs to speak to you in the present. It may be a passage that has spoken to you powerfully in the past – but is that the message for today? Perhaps it is, but you will need to discern this in prayer.

Ideally, you need to try to express this *in one sentence.* Any more than one sentence and you are probably trying to say too much for one sermon. But that one sentence will sum up what it is you believe God wants to say to the congregation *today.* It will be immediate, relevant and it will demand or encourage a response.

It is worth taking the time to make this sentence clear and memorable, since you may want to use it as part of the sermon itself, possibly repeating it more than once. You may decide to use your single-sentence message in the introduction, to make clear at the beginning what the sermon is to be about, or to draw the threads of the sermon together in the conclusion. Or you might decide to use it as a refrain to mark off or introduce your separate points. In the next section I give an example sermon where the single-sentence message is, 'The way we listen determines the way that we live.' I could choose to use this sentence as many as five times, marking off each separate point, reminding the congregation of what I most want them to learn.

Whether or not you include your single sentence in the sermon itself, it will keep your preparation on track. One of the hardest parts of preparation is to know what to leave out: which of the many ideas that come to mind don't fit in this particular sermon. Your single-sentence message will help you to decide on the points you want to make and to choose the illustrations that really convey this message and not some other.

The intention: knowing why you want to say it

The sermon is a spoken event. The spoken word always has an intention behind it. So what is your intention? What do you want your sermon to *do*?

- It may simply be to teach. You may want your congregation to understand some aspect of the Christian faith more clearly, or to make the connection between faith and some aspect of daily life. Teaching is often part of and the basis for the other possible intentions listed here.
- Perhaps you judge that the greatest need today is encouragement. Possibly the sermon is going to speak *for* the congregation more than *to* them, affirming their experience and showing them God's perspective.
- Or perhaps you want to challenge. Christian faith disrupts many of our comfortable certainties, challenges us to recognize our sinful tendencies and asks for costly and sometimes sacrificial love.
- Or will the tone of your sermon be one of warning? Is there a particular tendency like gossip or complacency that needs addressing?
- Or do you want to leave people excited? To open their minds and hearts to possibilities they may not have recognized? Some aspects of Christian faith, like the resurrection and the gift of the Holy Spirit, are stirring and exciting and it is good if the tone of the sermon can reflect this.
- Or your intention may be to guide, or comfort, or exhort . . .

It is vital to know what your intention will be. The intention behind the sermon gives it a consistent tone: what the rhetoricians call 'pathos'. And it is even more important than the content in helping you to choose the right illustrations: stories that comfort, or warn, or excite.

The intention will also help you in another of the more difficult phases of preparation: framing the conclusion. You will not want to bring a challenging sermon to a comforting end, or include a warning if your intention was simply to teach. The conclusion is an intensification of the message as a whole, so if you mean to challenge, you will need to choose challenging phrases for the conclusion; if the intention is to teach, make sure that you provide a clear summary of your message; if it is to inspire, you will look for an inspiring illustration or the kind of language that inspires.

The intention also acts as a check in another way. It gives you a clue as to why you chose this message in the first place. Why did you choose the encouraging message in the text rather than the potential challenge? Was this because you judged encouragement to be more important for the church on this occasion, or because you didn't feel confident about offering them a challenge? If you chose a challenging sermon, why was this? Was it because this is the way you tend to see the Christian life? Or are you, perhaps, frustrated with the congregation and wanting to shake them up a bit? Reflecting on the intention we have chosen can help us to judge how well we are listening to God or whether we are being driven by our own preoccupations, not only in our preaching but in our whole ministry.

It is, however, possible to have more than one intention. For example, you may want to both teach *and* encourage. Or you may be aware that something that is a challenge to one person may be an encouragement to someone else. But beware of having too many intentions, or simply leaving it to chance. In that case, just as with the lack of a single-sentence summary of the content, the sermon will be without focus.

The outcome: discerning how God may be calling people to respond

The goal of our preaching is transformation, both of the congregation and of individuals. What difference do you *expect* your sermon to make? A sermon that makes no difference dishonours the word of God, which is 'living and active, sharper than a two-edged sword' (Hebrews 4.12). So, bearing this in mind, what difference do you *want* your sermon to make? As in the case of the content and the intention, to aim at nothing is to be sure to hit it! And as with the intention, discerning how God may be calling people to respond will help you maintain a consistent tone, choose your illustrations and shape your conclusion.

- It may be a *definite action*, such as trying out a particular pattern of prayer; giving more generously, as in a sermon on stewardship; or evaluating their moral conduct, such as avoiding gossip.
- It may be a *change of attitude*. For example, you may want to contradict the attitude of the popular press about asylum seekers by reminding them of Israel's responsibility to welcome the stranger and Jesus' welcome of the outcast. Or you may want to emphasize the importance of wonder in our response to creation.

- It may be a *new framework of interpretation.* You may want people to realize that God is interested in our daily work; or to recognize our participation in Holy Communion as an expression of Christian community.

The response you are looking for may be from people as individuals or it may be from the congregation as a whole. You may want to exhort the church as the Christian community in that place to recognize the importance of its mission or to become more forgiving towards one another. Since we grow as disciples in community, a response from the whole church can be expected to have important effects on each individual member.

But it is important to remember that whatever response you expect or hope for from individuals depends on their situation at the time. As Jesus' parable of the sower makes clear, there are a thousand things that can prevent them from hearing the message. They may be struggling in their faith, coping with personal tragedy or anxiety, or feeling hurt by an ill-chosen remark. As a preacher it is rarely possible to take all these possibilities into account. The hoped-for outcome we decide on depends on circumstances beyond our control for its realization. But this is not a reason for not being aware of the difference your sermon might make to those in a position to give attention and respond.

Although I have placed it third for ease of explanation, discerning God's intention and expressing this as a hoped-for outcome of the sermon is actually of primary importance. The purpose of preaching is transformation. Its outcome should be change of some kind. Our hope should be that over time the congregation should be formed in the pattern of Christ. And it is to be hoped that a congregation will become used to applying the sermon practically and faithfully, so that even in difficult times individuals will discern in your sermon something that speaks to their present circumstances.

Discerning your message is the first stage in the creation of the sermon. To find a message each week that is fresh and lively and relevant for your congregation requires you to bring together your knowledge of several different areas. But knowledge alone is not enough. The way we know anything or anyone is conditioned by the way we love.

Know and love the Bible
Many churches follow a lectionary providing either two or three readings for every Sunday of the year, depending on whether the

service includes Holy Communion. In this case the readings are provided for you. A set lectionary has several advantages, the chief of which for you as the preacher is that it will force you to preach from time to time on little-known and sometimes difficult passages! Don't shy away from these. They are a wonderful discipline and often lead to surprising discoveries.

It's important to remember that you are not expected to preach on more than one of the set readings at a time. Hearing the Scripture read aloud has a value for a congregation regardless of whether the preacher adds anything to the passage. It is usually best to major on just one of the set passages, referring to others only in passing.

An exception to this rule may be on occasions where there is a major difficulty in a passage you have chosen not to preach on. Perhaps the Old Testament passage is a story of warfare or murder or the Gospel includes some particularly challenging words of Jesus and you judge that these may cause puzzlement or dismay. In that case, you might take a few minutes to address the difficulty before going on to your main message.

Between Advent and Pentecost the lectionary concentrates on the story of salvation through Jesus' life, death, resurrection and gift of the Spirit. But in 'ordinary time' after Pentecost there is freedom to preach through a particular book of the Bible or to frame a series of sermons around a theme. After six months concentrating on the great doctrinal truths of Christian faith it may be important during this time to be sure that you are addressing the issues of everyday life in your preaching. At any time it may be right to interrupt the regular course of readings for special events: a general election, a national or local tragedy, perhaps even a notable sporting achievement.

Having chosen a passage on which to preach, you need to let it speak to you. Don't go to the commentaries too soon. Listen to the text and hear what it is saying to you in your own life, before you decide what it might be saying to the congregation. Then spend as much time as you need in study, to be sure that you understand the passage well enough to preach on it to this particular congregation.

To do this effectively, you need to be in the habit of reading the Bible in your own devotional life and making space for it to speak to you in your immediate circumstances. Unless we ourselves are being transformed by listening to God's word through the Bible, it is idle to expect the congregation to be transformed through our preaching. Unless we love the Bible, making it a valued companion, we will be unable to convey such a love to others.

Know and love the congregation

You cannot expect to preach effectively if you don't know your congregation. And you will not get to know them unless you love them. Nor will the congregation give you authority as a preacher and be open to listen to what you say unless you love them. In the words of John Maxwell, 'People don't care how much you know until they know how much you care' (1993, p. 7). Moreover, without love you will not be able to get the message for your sermons week by week. Only if you love your congregation will you be able to hear from God what he wants to say to them. Only if you love them will you have the authority to say the hard things that may be necessary from time to time.

This also means letting people get to know you, for which you need to meet them in their homes, chat about their daily lives, know the problems that face them in work and family life. Some pastors, whose full-time work is Christian ministry, occasionally spend a morning or even a whole day at work with members of their congregation, getting to know them in the setting where they spend so much of their lives, gaining insights into the problems they face day by day. Without mentioning particular people and situations, except with their permission, all this information will help you when seeking to apply the message of the Bible to situations in people's everyday lives. Any preaching ministry is built on a foundation of pastoral care and concern in which you learn to love the people who listen to your sermons week by week and they learn to respect and trust you.

No congregation is homogeneous so generalizations may easily catch you out. But you will need to know about your congregation's general level of understanding of the Bible so as to judge for any given passage how much background information they need in order to understand it. You will need to know about the makeup of the congregation: do they come from similar or diverse backgrounds? Do they have similar or varying levels of education? Are they of much the same income group or are there wide divergences? You will need to know the 'style' of faith prevalent in the church. Do people tend to believe a person in authority such as you; or do they expect to believe only when they have the chance to think something out for themselves?

You will need to know too something about the history of the church: the stories that are told about the past, the people who are specially recalled and the qualities for which they are remembered, and in particular any shared times of joy or sorrow, success or struggle.

Know and love the community

Your congregation are part of a wider community whose life both you and they share, and it is important for you to know this community. You will need to keep up with local news and gossip through the local paper and talking to people in the streets. You will need to build relationships with the important people in the community, whoever they may be. You will need to know the outlines of its history and the factors which have shaped it. Your understanding of the community will also grow if you take funerals, since you will regularly hear the real-life stories of local people of all kinds. Depending on your situation, the divisions of your community, its history, injustices and aspirations may become important themes in your preaching.

It is valuable to make a habit of reading the newspaper or observing the local community with one ear open to what God may be saying. This discipline means that when it comes to applying the message of Scripture in our sermons, we are in familiar territory and are sharing from a rich storehouse of insights gained through regular reflection.

Know and love yourself

Each of the Old Testament prophets had a distinctive style and God chose each one of them, with their strengths and weaknesses, faults and foibles. You too have a particular style and it is important to recognize this. That style does not override any of the advice in this chapter: being a spontaneous person does not mean you can do without a structure in your sermons, and preferring abstract thinking (like me!) does not mean you don't need to look for arresting and evocative visual images. But if you love novels, for example, feel free to quote them and use incidents from them as illustrations, though you will need to make sure your congregation are on the same wavelength. If you are a sports-person, use sporting illustrations, but take care to avoid tiring the congregation with too many. If you are an enthusiastic person, let this come over; if gentle, be gentle in your preaching. Use your own style of humour rather than someone else's: if you are not good at telling jokes don't think you have to use them just because telling jokes is in fashion in some circles. The advice in this chapter is intended to describe what you need to strive for: apart from this, be yourself!

There are also several things to take into account about yourself when seeking to discern the message for your sermon. You will need to recognize your own hobbyhorses, and avoid riding them too often! You will need to be aware of the issues you are struggling with. It is a common mistake of preachers to be drawn to the topics they happen to be wrestling with at the time, but this rarely makes for effective preaching.

If possible you need to know the level of your authority. Your ability to challenge or warn or deliver difficult teaching depends on whether the congregation in general trusts you to have their best interests at heart. Preachers are flawed human beings like everyone else, and yet God chooses to make himself known in and through their words. But he is better able to do this when the preacher is aware of his failings and doesn't mind acknowledging them.

The listening preacher

Long ago the unknown prophet of the exile spoke about his own experience as a preacher: 'The LORD God has given me the tongue of a teacher, that I may know how to sustain the weary with a word. Morning by morning he wakens – he wakens my ear to listen as those who are taught' (Isaiah 50.4). To be a preacher it is necessary first to be a listener: to listen to God in the Bible, listen to the congregation, the community and to oneself.

And the most important piece in the jigsaw of discernment through which you will arrive at the message is prayer. Thus you will learn to hear the voice of the Holy Spirit. It is important not to presume what God wants to say. Sometimes there may be an obvious message in the text, clearly relevant for the congregation. But check it out: it may be that the obvious message is the right one, but perhaps not. Possibly there is something else that God wants to say on this occasion.

Personally, I am an intuitive person. I know when I have arrived at the message for a sermon because there is a deep sense of rightness about it. Sometimes in my reading a particular phrase or sentence in the Bible passage 'lights up' and is clearly the aspect that the Holy Spirit is pointing to. Sometimes I only discover afterwards why a sermon or part of a sermon was the message for the occasion.

Not everyone is the same and you may have a different way of knowing whether you have arrived at the message. Whatever is the case, learn to trust your sense of rightness as you learn to listen to the voice of the Holy Spirit.

EXERCISE 3A

The readings for 'Proper 23' in year C of the Church of England lectionary are as follows:

Jeremiah 29.1, 4–7; 2 Timothy 2.8–15; Luke 17.11–19

For each of these readings here are *two* possible messages, each with its single-sentence content, intention and hoped-for outcome:

Jeremiah 1:	content: 'God has a plan for us even in tragedy and bewilderment' intention: encourage outcome: have faith in God's presence in bad times as well as good.
Jeremiah 2:	content: 'Seek the welfare of the city' intention: teach and challenge outcome: recognize the vocation of daily work as serving the community on God's behalf.
2 Timothy 1:	content: 'A worker approved by God' intention: inspire outcome: make our relationship with God first priority in ministry.
2 Timothy 2:	content: 'If you can't bear a cross you won't wear a crown' intention: challenge outcome: recognize the inevitability of sharing Christ's suffering.
Luke 1:	content: 'If you are truly saved, you will be a worshipper' intention: challenge outcome: make regular worship a priority.
Luke 2:	content: 'Jesus showed grace to the thankless' intention: teach and encourage outcome: recognize God's grace as overflowing generosity.

For 'Proper 24' the readings are as follows:

Jeremiah 31.27–34; 2 Timothy 3.14—4.5; Luke 18.1–8

For each of these passages, work out *two* possible messages for your congregation, each with its single sentence, intention and outcome.

Exercise 3B

Devise a message with its single sentence, intention and outcome based on Colossians 3.12–17 for each of the following occasions:

- a Sunday in Lent
- the wedding of a couple in their twenties
- the funeral of an eminent local politician
- the church's anniversary celebration
- the dedication of a new community hall.

References

John Maxwell, 1993. *Developing the Leader Within You*. London: Nelson.

Further reading

Fred Craddock, 1985. *Preaching*. Nashville, Tennessee: Abingdon Press, Chapter 5: 'Interpretation: the listeners'.

David Day, 1998. *A Preaching Workbook*. London: SPCK, Part II: 'Discerning a message'.

Andy Stanley and Lane Jones, 2006. *Communicating for a Change*. Colorado Springs, Colorado: Multnomah Books, Chapter 12: 'Pick a point'.

Leonora Tubbs Tisdale, 1997. *Preaching as Local Theology and Folk Art*. Minneapolis, Minnesota: Fortress Press, Chapter 4: 'Preaching as local theology'.

The elements of structure

The importance of structure

The first stage in sermon preparation is getting the message: knowing *what* you want to say. The next is deciding *how* best to say it: giving your sermon a structure. Once you reach the point of discerning the message for the sermon, the next step is to decide how to structure it in order to convey that message.

A structure is to a sermon like a skeleton to a body: it provides the support and keeps the various parts in place, but is largely invisible. The congregation should sense that your sermon has structure: that you are able to move smoothly from point to point without getting lost. But they should not be distracted by it: it is the message they need to be aware of, not the structure.

In music, the baroque and classical composers like Bach and Mozart, working within the established forms of their time, produced a wide variety of beautiful pieces. In the same way, using a basic structure in preaching need not be restrictive. The same structure can be used for a wide variety of messages. In later periods of music, composers began to push the boundaries of musical form. But all the forms they used had to comply with the underlying structure of music. In this section we are going to work within one traditional, well-defined sermon structure. In the next we will look at how to work with structures of different kinds, but all must obey the basic rules of communication.

Making sure that your sermon has a structure has value, first for you, the preacher:

- It keeps your preparation on track, helping you to decide what to include, what to leave out and how to arrange what you want to say.
- It helps to maintain your focus on the message you have decided on.
- It makes the sermon easier to remember while you are preaching, making it less likely that you will get lost in your notes.
- It also makes it easier to decide which parts to miss out if the sermon turns out to be running on for too long or if you find you have to make changes at the last minute.

Equally important, a clear structure helps the congregation to listen:

- It helps them to follow you as you move from section to section.
- It helps them to understand your message.
- And it helps them to remember the sermon afterwards.

The four elements

In this section we are going to work with the traditional 'deductive' sermon structure. This is where you state your message at the beginning, develop the message in the main body of the sermon, and restate it in the conclusion. It has been summed up as: 'First tell 'em what you're going to tell 'em; then tell 'em; then tell 'em what you've told 'em.' The deductive structure is traditional and still very widely used. In fact, given the variety of possible structures available, it is probably used too often. Nevertheless it is a good place to start, since every preacher needs to know how to use this basic structure.

Whichever structure you use, your sermon will have four elements. They will be:

- an introduction
- interpretation of the Bible text
- application of the text
- a conclusion.

We are going to look in more detail at the introduction and the conclusion later on, so for now I will simply summarize the content and purpose of each.

In the introduction, you:

- establish rapport with the congregation;
- tell them what the sermon is going to be about;
- suggest why the sermon might be relevant to them;
- suggest how they might listen in order to get the full benefit of the sermon.

In the conclusion, you:

- provide a summary of your message;
- suggest why the message should matter to them;
- describe the difference it could make to them.

The last two points of the conclusion relate to the intention of your sermon and its desired outcome. The value of the sermon to your congregation – why it matters to them – will depend on your intention, whether it is to teach, encourage, challenge, etc. The difference it could make depends on the outcome you are hoping for, such as a new framework of understanding or some concrete action.

It helps to think of the introduction and conclusion as 'elements' rather than 'sections'. Usually, the introduction comes at the beginning and the conclusion at the end, like sections. But it is possible to move parts of both introduction and conclusion around. For example, you might include something whose aim is to build rapport, like a personal story, later in the sermon. And you might summarize your message several times rather than only once in the conclusion. But you will want to be sure that all the necessary parts of both introduction and conclusion are included somewhere.

Interpreting the Bible passage

Before embarking on this section it is as well to express a caveat. Millions of words have been expended on the science of biblical interpretation and it is impossible to do justice to them in the confines of a few paragraphs. In what follows I have separated out what some will know as the two 'horizons': the meaning of the text for its original audience and the meaning of the text for today. I freely admit that this is a simplification. In practice, our sense of the meaning of a text for today deeply affects our understanding of what it might have meant when originally written. In addition, the text's 'original' meaning may be obscure or the subject of debate. I nevertheless believe that it is important to distinguish between these two 'horizons' and to be honest with ourselves about the connections we make between them. I explain in a bit more detail why this is so in what follows.

Interpreting the passage means explaining its meaning for the original audience. Immediately the question arises: which 'original' audience? Usually it is clear who the original audience was: the recipients of one of Paul's letters, for example. Sometimes, however, you will know from your critical study of the passage that there is more than one possible 'original audience'. For the Gospels, for example, there are at least two possibilities: the people in the Gospel stories who heard Jesus teach and experienced the miracles, or the early church for which the Gospel was intended as teaching and to build their faith. For a passage from the prophets, it might be the people who heard the original message or the readers of the book in its final form. And even for Paul's letters, were these written to be heard by *individuals* or by the *community*? In many cases I suggest that you are free to decide, depending on the message you have chosen, but it will be important for you to be clear in your own mind which audience you are working with.

According to some contemporary approaches to interpretation, it is not necessary to ask about the original audience. We simply listen to the text and ask what it is saying to us. My personal opinion is that you can't take this approach to preaching without a loss of integrity. The reason is that both preacher and congregation stand in a tradition in which the words and actions of God have been received and interpreted over the centuries. They have been interpreted within a community called and set apart for God under the guidance of the Holy Spirit. It is through this process of theological reflection that both the Bible itself came into existence and the living word of God addresses us in the present. To dispense with the meaning of the text to its original audience is to cut ourselves off from this living tradition of interpretation. We may be hearing something striking and even life-changing but it is doubtful whether what we hear will be the word of God. It will be like a text torn out of its context and made to say whatever the preacher or listener wishes it to say. For this reason I am going to assume that you will want to pay attention to the interpretation of the passage.

In order to interpret the passage, you will need to put yourself into the congregation's shoes, which is why it is so important that you have grown to know and love them. I suggest that you will want to ask three questions:

What background information will they need in order to make sense of the passage?

For example, if the passage includes an encounter between Jesus and the Pharisees, how much do they know about the Pharisees and how much do they need to know? That they were Jesus' opponents? That they were very strict in keeping the Law? That they were thought of as particularly 'good' people?

The golden rule here is to give as much information as your congregation needs but not to overwhelm them with too much. You may know from your own study that some scholars think the Pharisees have been given a rather bad press in the Gospels and presented as a stereotype. Whether your congregation need to know this depends on the message of the sermon. It may be relevant on this occasion; it may not.

What potential difficulties and stumbling-blocks are there in these passages?

You may judge that you need to address these regardless of whether they are relevant to your message. For example, when Jesus told his followers to 'hate' their families, did he really mean this? Or when he said to his mother, 'What have you to do with me, woman?' was he being rude? In both these cases, the answer is quite straightforward: these were Semitic forms of speech, which sound harsh to our ears. In other cases, more explanation may be required.

In some cases a difficulty in the passage may lie at the heart of your message. For example, preaching on the parable of the great feast in Matthew 22.1–14, the severity of the king towards both his servants and his enemies struck me as a difficulty, especially if we take the king as a portrayal of the risen, reigning Christ. I dealt with the severity of the king towards his enemies by explaining the context of the readers of Matthew's Gospel, under pressure of rejection and persecution by the Jews, showing that this was a prediction of the destruction of the Temple. I used his severity towards the servants as the starting point for the message 'The grace of God calls us to changed lives', exploring the demand of the gospel against the background of costly grace.

How can I set the scene?

Having put yourselves in your congregation's shoes to spot the background they may need and the difficulties they may need clearing up, you now turn to your main task: setting the scene. What you will be aiming to do is to explain the context for the message in a creative way.

The key to this is the use of the imagination to evoke feelings as well as to supply the necessary information. You may want your congregation to feel the sun on their backs and hear the sound of the waves breaking on the beach as they sit on the shore of the Sea of Galilee listening to Jesus teaching, or to empathize with Paul's frustration as well as to understand his dilemma in addressing the factious and independent-minded Corinthians. Or to experience the despair of the exiles to whom the prophet addresses a message of hope.

In relation to interpretation you are the expert. You have been trained to interpret the Bible, and as pastor, leader and teacher you are sharing with the congregation the benefit of that training. It is vital that in doing so you don't distance them from the Bible, making it appear that only an expert can possibly interpret it correctly. Rather, you need to aim to whet their appetite, increasing their desire to read it for themselves, providing guidelines on how to approach it.

The key to doing this may well be that you *expect* them to be reading the Bible for themselves. Then you may find yourself including phrases like, 'When you come across a passage like this' or 'I wonder what you make of this?' In our whole preaching ministry, we need to model a confidence in approaching the Bible and an expectation that it will speak to us. In this way we encourage our congregation to make friends with the Bible, reading it regularly for themselves, rather than remaining on a distant, nodding acquaintance.

Applying the Bible passage

Application is the context for our whole preaching ministry. The whole point is to play our part in the transformation God wants to bring about in the lives of individuals and congregations. And listeners want application. They want to know that the Bible has relevance to their lives.

However, in relation to interpretation you are the expert: when it comes to application you may not be. Your authority is that of leader or pastor and so depends on your relationship with the congregation. Just as the good preacher will use his expertise to draw the congregation into a relationship with the Bible rather than distance them from it, so the good preacher will use his authority wisely to involve the congregation in the process of application rather than dictate what this should be.

Application of a passage from the Bible to everyday life depends on the answers to three questions:

1 What situations might the passage address today?
2 What might the passage have to say to those situations?
3 How might the congregation in those situations respond?

The passage might be applied to several different kinds of situations:

- *In the life of the congregation itself.* You might want the congregation to avoid gossip, support one another, understand the service of Holy Communion better, become more involved in the mission of God . . . or any one of a host of other possible outcomes. In these cases you are acting as teacher, pastor and leader, suggesting how the church might respond to the particular passage *as a church*. To achieve this it is important to be aware of your authority within the congregation and its limits so that your leadership remains effective. You may be aware that the Bible calls for certain standards of behaviour, such as in sexual morality, mutual forgiveness or hospitality to the stranger, which members of your congregation do not share. In such cases you need to make the basis for your judgements very clear and commend them with an appropriate humility without compromising what you believe the passage to demand.
- *To a situation in which you and they are on an equal footing*, such as local or national life: a major natural disaster, a controversial decision of the local council, and so on. Here again, you speak with the authority of a Christian pastor or leader, suggesting how Christians might understand or respond. But depending on the situation you may need to be tentative and humble, allowing room for disagreement or suggesting a variety of possible applications.
- *To a situation in which they are the experts*, such as their daily life and work. Perhaps it is because so many preachers are intuitively

aware that they cannot speak as experts in this field that sermons on work and daily life are so rare. And yet if we avoid applying the Bible to the working lives of our congregation, is it any wonder if they decide that Christianity is irrelevant to daily life? In Chapter 4, I suggest how the congregation might be involved in this area of application through interactive preaching. Alternatively, it is becoming gradually more common for preachers to convene sermon groups to explore the issues their congregation face in daily life so that they are better able to address them in their preaching. But even without taking this step it is possible to encourage our listeners to take away a message for their everyday working lives. Ideally, we want to invite and encourage them to engage in a process of reflection for themselves.

The more successfully you are able to connect your preaching to the process of theological reflection already taking place in the church, the more effective it will be and the better people are likely to remember your sermons. This is not easy to achieve, but here are some suggestions:

- Make it clear that you expect people to be reflecting. Use phrases like, 'As you reflect on this message . . .' and 'I wonder . . .'
- When describing a situation, include feelings and other details that help people unfamiliar with it to 'enter the situation'. Doing this helps them to become intuitively more aware of how the message of the Bible passage might apply.
- Highlight examples of theological reflection in Scripture. My wife Meg once preached about the centurion who came to Jesus to ask for healing for his slave (Luke 7.1–10). Her point was not about the healing. It concerned the way the centurion made the connection between his own authority and that of Jesus. Not only did he use his familiar work situation as a springboard to faith, but what he saw in Jesus affirmed his own daily exercise of authority.
- Avoid being dogmatic in your application: be aware there is more than one way of applying a principle. Be clear about the principle, where appropriate, but encourage people to apply it for themselves.
- Similarly, when using an illustration, make it clear that this shows one way of applying the message, but probably not the only one.
- Use illustrations of people who arrived at a conclusion through reflection.

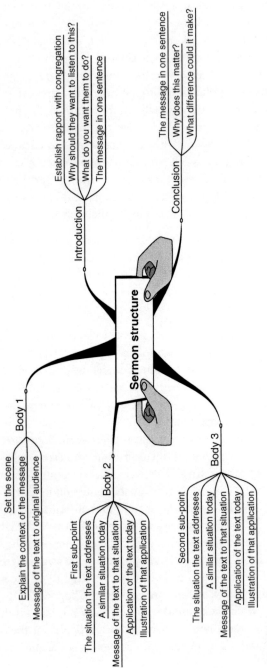

Figure 3.1

Integrating interpretation and application

I have emphasized that interpretation and application are not sections so much as elements of the sermon. The most important reason for this is that in practice you will probably move between interpretation and application several times. Figure 3.1 shows the structure of a typical deductive sermon.

- The introduction includes a statement of the message, which is then developed in the body of the sermon.
- Point 1 sets the scene and uses this to explain the message of the text to its original audience, placing that message in its context.
- Point 2 takes an aspect of the message, showing how it applied in its original situation, then suggesting a situation to which the text might apply today, perhaps with an illustration.
- Point 3 takes another aspect of the message and does the same thing.
- The conclusion then restates the message and intensifies it, demonstrating its importance and suggesting the difference it could make.

With this structure, as with almost any such deductive structure, you will be switching between the two 'horizons', the message in its original context and the message for today. The golden rule is to do this enough to maintain the congregation's interest and attention but not so much that you confuse them. This is a judgement that you make based on your knowledge of your congregation. It will also depend on the type of structure you are using. In a narrative structure, for example, there can be scope to change horizons more often: you might set a Bible story alongside a story from the present day, switching between them several times to apply the message.

Figure 3.2 is a fully worked example based on the parable of the sower in Mark 4.1–20. Jesus' words to the crowd both begin and end with the word, 'Listen!' His explanation to the disciples also highlights their ability and responsibility to hear the message and respond to it. As in both the parallels, Matthew 13.1–23 and Luke 8.4–15, the subject of this parable is the response to Jesus' ministry as a whole. In some ways it is a parable about parables. It is this that I have chosen to make the focus of the sermon.

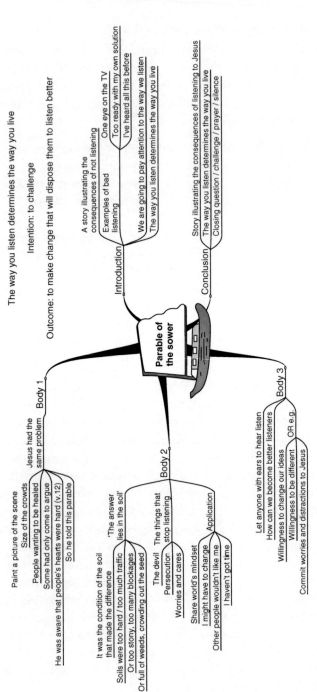

The way you listen determines the way you live

Intention: to challenge

Outcome: to make change that will dispose them to listen better

Parable of the sower

Introduction
- A story illustrating the consequences of not listening
  - Examples of bad listening
    - One eye on the TV
    - Too ready with my own solution
    - I've heard all this before
  - We are going to pay attention to the way we listen
  - The way you listen determines the way you live

Conclusion
- Story illustrating the consequences of listening to Jesus
- The way you listen determines the way you live
- Closing question / challenge / prayer / silence

Body 1
- Paint a picture of the scene
  - Size of the crowds
  - People wanting to be healed
  - Some had only come to argue
- Jesus had the same problem
- He was aware that people's hearts were hard (v.12)
- So he told this parable

Body 2
- It was the condition of the soil that made the difference
- 'The answer lies in the soil'
  - Soils were too hard / too much traffic
  - Or too stony, too many blockages
  - Or full of weeds, crowding out the seed
- The things that stop listening
  - The devil
  - Persecution
  - Worries and cares
- Application
  - Share world's mindset
  - I might have to change
  - Other people wouldn't like me
  - I haven't got time

Body 3
- Let anyone with ears to hear listen
- How can we become better listeners
  - Willingness to change our ideas
  - Willingness to be different
  - OR e.g.
  - Commit worries and distractions to Jesus

Figure 3.2

The *content of the message in one sentence* is, 'The way you listen determines the way you live.'

The *intention* is to introduce a note of challenge, just as in the case of Jesus.

And the *outcome I hope for* is that people will evaluate the way they listen or fail to listen and make some changes that will enable them to become better listeners.

Introduction

I might begin by telling a story about myself in which I failed to listen properly, with unfortunate results. By making the story about myself I establish rapport with the congregation by admitting that I have problems in this area too. I also highlight the importance of listening. Then I give some further examples of ways in which we might listen badly. I will then say that in this sermon we are going to pay attention to the way we listen. By saying this I have alerted the congregation to *how* I want them to listen to the sermon. Finally, the introduction ends with a statement of the message in one sentence: 'The way you listen determines the way you live.'

There is an element of anticipation in the way I have formulated this sentence: it is not immediately obvious why this should be so, but I am hoping that the congregation will want to pay attention in order to find out.

Main body: point 1

I might begin this point by saying that Jesus encountered the same problem: he knew that people were not very good listeners. Then I go on to paint a word picture of the scene: the crowds on the shore of the lake in the hot sun, some of them chatting among themselves, others distracted by fractious children, some who have come to be healed only waiting until Jesus has finished in order to approach him, others who have come to argue, and just a few straining forward to catch every word. Jesus knew that people encounter barriers to listening from both within and without, and this is the context for the parable. Its message is, 'The way you listen determines the way you live.'

Main body: point 2

Rather than take each type of soil one by one, I have decided to include all four kinds of soil under one heading. Partly this is because I don't have time to talk about all four individually. I also judge that my single-sentence message applies in the same way to all four: all four are examples of how we listen, or fail to listen. So, as Kenneth Williams used to say in the radio programme *Beyond our Ken*, 'The answer lies in the soil.' It was the condition of the soil that made the difference: either too hard, or too stony, or full of weeds, or just right for the seed. The amount of description will depend on the time available. If there is enough time, I might dwell on the casual tramping feet, the hostile environment of the stony soil, the competition of the weeds, and the farmer's disappointment when the seed he had sown failed to grow or ripen.

Jesus tells us that the things that stop the seed growing in the parable stand for the work of the devil, persecution and the worries and cares of life. Now I need to apply this to the present day. What situations might correspond to the ones Jesus talked about? Here, as in all application, I want my congregation to be thinking along with me. I don't want just to tell them what the application is; rather, I might suggest or raise questions. Are there situations where we share the world's mindset that prevent us from understanding Jesus? Are we afraid that if we take this seriously other people might not like us, or will think we are cranks? Are we anxious that we might have to change, or that we might be called on to give up more of our precious time than we would like?

Main body: point 3

Point 1 consisted entirely of interpretation, point 2 was balanced between interpretation and application; point 3 consists almost entirely of application. It aims to answer the question: 'What might make us better listeners?' Do we need to become more willing to change, more willing to be different from others, more ready to seek God's help in times of anxiety and stress? The overall point is that listening is not easy and there are changes we need to make if we are to listen more effectively to Jesus.

Conclusion

The conclusion begins with a story illustrating the consequences of listening to Jesus. A lot is hanging on this story. It is the culmination of the whole sermon. It suggests both why this subject might be so important and the kind of difference it might make. But if I can find the right story, or even make one up, I may achieve my aim and leave the congregation ready to consider changing.

After the story, there is no need to stretch the sermon out. I repeat the message one final time and then, because the intention of the sermon is to challenge, finish on a note of challenge, perhaps a question for people to consider and a suitable pause for silence.

EXERCISE 3C

Take one or more of the messages that you developed in either Exercise 3A or 3B, with its single-sentence content, intention and outcome.

Using a simple deductive structure, create an outline for the main body of the sermon. Divide the body of the sermon into as many points as you think appropriate (three is usually the maximum).

Pay attention to interpretation (the horizon of the original audience) and application (the horizon of the present day) but make sure you don't move between these horizons too often for comfort.

Points to be aware of about interpretation

- Your basic question is: 'What did this text mean in its original context?'
- You need to say enough to help your congregation understand this, but not so much that you blind them with science (in this case the science of biblical interpretation).
- Ask questions like:
  - ➤ How are they going to 'hear' this passage? Is it familiar/unfamiliar? Will it come across as encouragement or challenge?
  - ➤ What is the context for the message of the passage?
  - ➤ How much background information do I need to give (and how much do they know already)?
  - ➤ What are the potential stumbling-blocks in the passage?
  - ➤ How will I set the scene?

Points to be aware of about application

- Ask what situations this passage might address. Help the congregation to enter that situation and *feel* what it is like; why should this situation be important enough for us to apply the Bible to it?
- Don't be dogmatic: there are usually several ways of applying a principle. If you use a story to illustrate one way, you might need to mention one or two other possibilities.
- If you use stories for illustrations make sure they really illustrate the point you are making.

Further reading

Fred Craddock, 1985. *Preaching*. Nashville, Tennessee: Abingdon Press, Chapter 6: 'Interpretation: the text'; Chapter 7: 'Interpretation: between text and listener'; Chapter 8: 'Qualities to be sought for in a sermon'.

David Day, 1998. *A Preaching Workbook*. London: SPCK, Part I: 'Hearing the word'.

David Day, 2005. 'Preaching the epistles', in David Day, Jeff Astley and Leslie J. Francis, eds, *A Reader on Preaching*. Farnham: Ashgate.

Andy Stanley and Lane Jones, 2006. *Communicating for a Change*. Colorado Springs, Colorado: Multnomah Books, Chapter 13: 'Create a map'.

The varieties of structure

In the previous section we looked at the use of structure as the skeleton of your sermon, providing an outline that keeps all the component parts in their proper place without drawing attention to itself. We employed a simple and commonly used structure to explore the four essential elements in any sermon structure: the introduction and conclusion, interpretation and application of the Bible passage. But this 'deductive' structure, beginning with a message based on the biblical text, is by no means the only possible approach. In fact there is a wide variety of structures and structural elements available. Knowing how to use these and how to choose the structure that best fits the passage you are preaching on and the message you want to give will help to keep your preaching fresh and interesting. It will also help you when it comes to constructing sermons week in, week out, among the multiple calls of ministry. Learning how to use a variety of structures is something that comes with time and practice, so the purpose of this section is to provide enough stimulation and guidance to get you started.

Inductive structure

'Inductive' preaching is associated particularly with Fred Craddock and his introduction of what was called the 'new homiletic'. Instead of beginning with the biblical text and a message that is then applied to the hearers' situation, Craddock advocated beginning with the situation. Thus an inductive sermon does not begin with a statement of the message. It begins with an exploration of a contemporary situation. Only when this situation has been thoroughly explored does the preacher refer to the Bible passage, drawing resources from the passage to speak to the situation: a biblical principle, an aspect of God's character, or perhaps simply a saying or action of Jesus, which the congregation can then apply.

An example may help to show more clearly the contrast between the two styles. We will take the parable of the great feast in Matthew 22, which I mentioned in the previous section. The theme of this parable might be understood as God's invitation. The message for the sermon, based on the theme of God's invitation, might vary depending on the congregation and the occasion. Here are two possibilities for sermons with deductive structure:

- The first possibility might be a sermon with an evangelistic thrust based around the message: 'God invites you to enter his kingdom', with the intention of teaching what a response to Jesus involves and the hope that some of the congregation might come to consider such a response. A three-point sermon, which is one of the most commonly used forms of deductive structure, might develop the points: God's invitation is open to all; demands priority; and requires changed lives.
- On the other hand, in the sermon I preached on this text, in which I took as my starting point the severity of the king towards his enemies and the man found without a wedding garment, the message was simply, 'The grace of God calls us to changed lives', with the intention of teaching this and offering a challenge to consider how God might be calling us to change. I began by explaining the text to address the difficulty, and then suggested how we might apply it.

In contrast to this, the *inductive* approach begins with a situation relevant to the congregation. It asks them to enter this situation, evokes the feelings that might be involved and explores the possibilities, only then going to the biblical text for guidance. Here are two possible examples:

- Suppose a particular congregation is facing an issue about the use of its buildings for a group of local teenagers, or seeking to become more open to and inclusive of children in its worship. Change of this kind may throw up a variety of feelings and responses. The young people don't look after the building: they leave it untidy; there may even be incidents of vandalism. Children make a noise in the services, making it more difficult for the regular worshippers to concentrate. There may be changes in the worship to accommodate them. The preacher will explore the situation; empathize with the feelings involved; explain the reasons for the change being attempted; and acknowledge the disadvantages and difficulties. The whole congregation, insofar as the members are interested and aware, is enabled to acknowledge the feelings that have been stirred up and the discomfort of change. What guidance does the passage offer to help them reflect on this situation? In the parable, all were invited to the feast, the outcasts and the disreputable as well as the 'insiders'. Such an open invitation offended and even scandalized many – and here the preacher might well explore the feelings of the Pharisees as they listened to Jesus. But there was an expectation of change. How can this congregation so act as to affirm its open invitation and provide support for people it finds difficult in the process of change?

- Alternatively, the situation may be that faced by individual members of the congregation in the course of their daily lives. What is really at stake in being a Christian? Is it simply a question of attending church on a Sunday and supporting church events? Or does being a Christian make a difference to the way we go about our daily work? Does it make a difference to our sexual morality, the way we spend our money? The preacher would instantiate these questions with examples drawn from his own life and the kinds of experience members of the congregation might share. He then asks: does Christian faith provide a framework of practical wisdom to help us live our lives in a consistent way? Surely it does so, and this is what the severity of the king in the parable may suggest. Like the images of the narrow gate and the steep road in Matthew 7, this parable in Matthew 22 seems to emphasize the demand of the kingdom.

In the previous chapter we looked at the learning cycle. There we saw that new learning always engages with our pre-existing framework of understanding, sometimes confirming and building on that framework, sometimes challenging it and inviting change. The cycle can begin at any point, but to be effective new learning must involve all the stages. It is not difficult to see that the deductive structure begins at the stage of concept formation. In a deductive sermon the preacher presents a concept, a principle or idea derived from the biblical passage, explains it and then seeks to apply it. If the congregation are to learn it fully, they will need to take it away and put it into practice, experience the results and reflect on them for themselves. The weakness of the deductive structure is that the preacher cannot guarantee that this will happen, with the result that, like the seed falling on the path in Jesus' parable, the word may be lost simply because it is never put into practice.

On the other hand, inductive preaching, like most of the informal theological reflection taking place in a congregation, begins with the experience stage of the cycle. It explores that experience – which is why it is important for the preacher to spend time on this part of the sermon, evoking feelings and exploring aspects of the situation, so that the congregation really enters it. It then suggests a concept that might apply to the situation, a way of understanding it in the light of the message of the Bible passage. Thus the inductive sermon, if it is well designed, has covered three of the four stages of the cycle. All that remains is for the congregation to act on the new framework of understanding offered.

A final example is taken from the parable of the rich man and Lazarus in Luke 16. In the Revised Common Lectionary, this was the Gospel reading for Back to Church Sunday in 2010. My daughter Naomi had been asked to preach and wondered how she was to make this story relevant to the specially invited guests, relatively unfamiliar with church, who she hoped might be there. I suggested an inductive structure, beginning by seeking to identify those aspects of the situation portrayed in the story she could reasonably expect anyone in her congregation to agree on: that the way the rich man behaved was fundamentally wrong, that wealth opens the door to a variety of good purposes, and that we live in a world of glaring inequality. Into this situation comes the message of the parable: that God hates injustice and selfishness and that he expects us to act on what we know to be right. In fact, God calls his Church to play an active role in opposing injustice in the world and this is part of what we stand for.

Both this example and the one above about the scope of Christian faith illustrate the importance of what Ann Morisy (2004) calls the foundational and vocational dimensions of faith, which unite those with a definite Christian faith with those uncertain about faith or searching. The foundational domain centres on the awareness of the possibility of God and the difference faith might make in the ordinary experience of life. It points us to the God-ward dimensions of the physical creation, from the structure of a flower to an inspiring view to the sight of the stars at night; or to the God-ward dimensions of relationships, the birth of a new baby, the felt depth in a shared experience, the loss of a loved one. The vocational domain speaks to the desire many people share to discover a better self, live a better, more worthwhile life, make a difference for the better. The disadvantage of a lectionary is that it can direct us week by week to what Morisy calls the 'explicit' domain of faith, understood by Christians alone. Preaching inductively, on the other hand, invites us to explore these foundational and vocational domains and through these to make vital connections between faith and daily life.

Here is an attempt to do that at the start of a brief funeral sermon, which addresses the fear of death:

Reading: John 14.1–6
Hymn: 'The Lord's my shepherd'
Message: Jesus offers the possibility of confidence in the face of death.
Intention: Teach and encourage.
Outcome: Understand an aspect of Christian hope.

> Yea though I walk through death's dark vale, yet will I fear none ill,
> for thou art with me, and thy rod and staff me comfort still.

Facing the possibility of death
 the first thing the writer talks about is fear
  many people are afraid of death
   don't talk about it, don't like to think about it.
There is a reason for fear
 death a door into the unknown
  death sets a term to all we hope and strive for
   separation from those we love.
But the psalmist is able to say: 'I'm not afraid
 because I know that God will be with me.'
  Jesus says to his disciples: 'Don't be worried and upset
   because I'm going to be with you.'

Continued . . .

Narrative structure

Another way of preaching is to tell a story. Just as inductive preaching goes with the grain of the informal theological reflection taking place in a congregation, narrative preaching reflects the fact that we experience our lives as a story, a story we are constantly trying to make sense of. A narrative approach to preaching invites us to become aware of the way we give meaning to our lives, or some aspects of them, and to consider these in the light of God's story.

A well-told story is easily memorable. To be able to remember the beginning, the end or some significant feature in the story usually offers the key to recalling the whole story. A story evokes feelings and imagination: it invites us to identify with one or more of the characters, to consider what we would have done in their place, to compare the actions they take or the meaning they make of the situation with what our own might have been. A story reveals character and invites us to make judgements on the characters we encounter. But stories are also open-ended: they do not hem us in. A story invites us to re-examine the way we think and feel about the world but does not require us to do so. No wonder the Bible is full of stories, through which we glimpse the character of God. No wonder Jesus made such use of stories in his teaching. And the Bible as a whole presents the story of God's people and invites us to make it our story, to let it form the way we understand and imagine the world.

Narrative might form the whole of the sermon, or the sermon may have a story embedded within it. It is possible to imagine several ways to use narrative:

- Retelling a Bible story. Typically, biblical narrative is fairly 'sparse', giving you plenty of opportunity to embroider the story, explain the context, tell it from several different points of view, insert feelings, invite the congregation to speculate on the motives of the characters, identify with one or more of them, and draw lessons from the outcome.
- Updating a Bible story. A tried and tested approach, which greatly depends on the preacher's awareness of the contemporary situation in which the updated story is set.
- Making up a story, whose characters or outcome help to illustrate or teach the message you want to bring from the passage.
- Telling a contemporary story and then a Bible story as a comparison or as a way of reflecting on the contemporary story.
- Running a Bible story and a contemporary story alongside each other, switching from one to the other from time to time.

It is also possible to combine inductive and narrative structures, especially if the biblical text is a narrative. We might begin by exploring the problem situation, highlighting the issues and the feelings that may arise, before showing that the text addresses these same issues and feelings but also brings a word from God for the situation.

Parable

Parable is a refinement of narrative preaching. Like straightforward story-telling, the whole sermon might be in the form of a parable or you might include an element of parable in a different structure, such as ending with an open question or open-ended story. I'm not particularly good at using parable, but here is an extract from a sermon in which I tried it. I judged that God's instructions to Adam and Eve in the Garden of Eden might easily be taken as unwelcome restriction, whereas the message I wanted to give was that in fact boundaries create freedom. Towards the beginning of the sermon I posed the question, 'How do you hear these words? As permission or restriction?' and I used variations on this question throughout the sermon to mark the transitions from one point to another. The two stories I used in the introduction were only completed at the end of the sermon, in a way I judged most of my hearers would not have expected, in order to reinforce the message.

Text: Genesis 2.4–9, 15–17
Message: A bounded life is a life of freedom.
Intention: Challenge.
Outcome: New/renewed way of thinking.

> The Lord God took the man and put him in the garden to till it and to keep it. And the Lord God commanded the man, 'You may freely eat of every tree of the garden; but of the tree of the knowledge of good and evil you shall not eat, for in the day you eat of it you shall die.'

How do you hear these words? As permission or restriction?
 there's a whole world out there waiting to be explored
  but God puts the first human being in a garden
   and tells him to stay there
    he can eat of any tree in the garden
     but not the interesting one in the middle
      and there is a dire threat to back up the command.

How do you hear this? As permission or restriction?

Some time ago some friends visited us, bringing their two young sons
when they arrived, after we greeted them
the mother gave the two boys a guided tour of our sitting room
you can sit on these chairs and that settee
you can play around and underneath this table
but you are not to touch the knobs on the audio
or press the buttons on the front of the TV
what do you think those two young lads did?
Back in the old days before the invention of health and safety
a primary school was renewing the fence around its playground
so one day the children came out for their mid-morning break
and found that the fence had been taken away
what do you expect the children would have done?

The sermon ended like this:

Restriction or permission?
freedom or limitation?
initiative or obedience?
or is it both?
is the Christian life in fact a bounded space
within which there is both initiative and permission?
I wonder if you remember those two stories I told at the beginning of
this sermon
let me tell you how they each turned out
the children in the playground all huddled together in the middle
and the two little boys played happily all the time they were with us.

There is a powerful essay by Eugene Peterson entitled 'The subversive pastor' (2002) in which he points out that many people have inbuilt defences against the truth. The reason they don't wish to change in response to the gospel is that the change would upset their comfortable lifestyle or complacent self-image. To people like this a straightforward challenge may be like water off a duck's back. The 'subversive' element in the use of parable is that the narrative structure draws people in, invites them to identify with a character or think and feel in a certain way, and then turns the tables on them with an unexpected outcome.

This is often, though not exclusively, the way Jesus used parables. His reason, as he explains to his disciples in Matthew 13.11–17, is that many of his hearers were hard of heart: they really did not want to accept his message. The explanation was for those willing to make a costly commitment in becoming his followers.

Structural elements

In his book *Preaching* Fred Craddock (1985) provides a list of possible sermon structures and invites us to think about the various ways in which these might be used:

- What is it? What is it worth? How does one get it?
- Explore, explain, apply
- The problem, the solution
- What it is, what it is not
- Either–or
- Both–and
- Promise, fulfilment
- Ambiguity, clarity
- Major premise, minor premise, conclusion
- Not this, nor this, nor this, but this
- Flashback (present to past to present)
- From the lesser to the greater.

In each case, it is possible to envisage these as structures for a whole sermon, but equally they might be thought of as 'structural elements' making up part of the sermon. Thus 'problem–solution', 'ambiguity–clarity' or 'flash-back' might form the structure of just one point in a longer sermon.

To suggest some examples, the theme of a sermon might be 'What is humility?' and the chosen structure 'Not this, or this, or this, but this'. Humility does not mean underestimating our gifts, nor does it mean lack of confidence; humility does not mean allowing ourselves to be used as a doormat; rather, humility is . . .

Another example might come from Matthew 6.24–33 on the difference between a 'scarcity mentality' and an 'abundance mentality', worrying about the future or trusting God to provide. Either/or might not be so much the structure of the sermon as a constantly recurring theme.

Structures for all occasions

The ability to use a variety of different structures is of huge value to the preacher. It not only prevents our preaching becoming stale or falling into a rut, it acts as a tool-box from which we can select the one most appropriate to the message, the passage and the situation. In a busy ministry, when preaching every week is only one of the many tasks to which we are called, it can act as a life-saver, keeping our preaching fresh and interesting. With experience the skilled preacher will be both like Bach and Mozart, able to compose many different sermons using a similar underlying structure, and like more modern composers, able to push the boundaries, shaping structure creatively to suit the message.

But the value of having several different structures at one's disposal goes further than this. The structure of a sermon, the way the message is conveyed, is itself part of the message. To use only one or two structures week by week will reinforce an underlying message about the Bible and its place in our lives:

- Deductive preaching presents the Bible as a manual for life and encourages the hearer to place confidence in its message. But overuse of this structure can tend to suggest that faith is cut and dried, that for every problem there is an instant solution.
- Inductive preaching balances this by suggesting that faith is not cut and dried, but that the Bible does supply resources to help us in the challenges of everyday life.
- 'Before–after' structure reminds the hearer that faith involves transformation, but overuse of it might suggest that instant conversion or decisive change is the norm.
- 'Either–or' reinforces the point that faith involves decision, but might equally suggest oversimplification or inflexibility.
- Whereas 'both–and' might help to broaden the congregation's horizons and sympathy but avoids confronting them with a decision.

Which structure is the passage calling for?

It may well be that the passage on which you have chosen to preach itself suggests an appropriate structure:

- In his letters, Paul often uses a deductive structure. He states the principle and then applies it. So for example, in the extended argument on food offered to idols in 1 Corinthians 8 to 10, he begins with a statement of the message: 'Knowledge puffs up, but love builds up'. In doing so, he is responding to the Corinthians' own, faulty, principle: 'We all have knowledge.' The rest of the three chapters is a warning against the danger of relying on knowledge alone to build the church and a reminder of the vital importance of love.

- If you were preaching on the story of the rich man in Mark 10.17–22 and many of the stories that portray the need for decision, an appropriate structure might be 'either–or': in the case of the man, either Jesus or wealth – what might it be in our own case?
- Preaching on the parables poses a challenge, and not just because many are so familiar. The message of these stories to their original audience was designed to challenge and shock. The preacher is faced with the task of deciding whether there might be an appropriate challenge for her own audience. And if so, perhaps the use of parable might itself become part of the sermon structure.
- On the other hand, many Bible passages are in narrative form. The book of Ruth is a story about the providence of God in an unlikely place and challenging circumstances. It draws the listener in and evokes sympathy with an outsider, Ruth the Moabite. A narrative structure might well be most faithful to the book's message and intention.

EXERCISE 3D

Use the passage you worked on for Exercise 3C, with the same message. In that exercise you created a deductive outline for the sermon. In this one the exercise is to create an alternative outline, either inductive or narrative.

If you choose an inductive structure, you might also use some of the structures from Fred Craddock's list as structural elements for part of the sermon. Alternatively, you could use one of these for the structure of the whole sermon. If you choose to begin with the situation, think of the way you will evoke feelings and ambiguity to help your imagined congregation 'enter' that situation.

A narrative sermon tells a story. The essence of good story-telling is concreteness, so include the incidental details that will help your congregation imagine the situation and put themselves into it.

- You might retell the biblical story, pausing for commentary at strategic points, or simply retell the story in such a way as to bring out the message you have decided on, and then apply it.
- Or you might tell a story of the present day and include in the story an application of the Bible passage.

It is part of the point of this exercise that you use the *same* passage, message content, intention and outcome, so that you experience the important principle that there are different ways of planning a sermon with the same message.

References

Ann Morisy, 2004. *Journeying Out*. London: Continuum.

Eugene Peterson, 2002. 'The subversive pastor', in *Life at its Best*. Grand Rapids, Michigan: Zondervan.

Further reading

David Buttrick, 2005. 'On preaching a parable', in David Day, Jeff Astley and Leslie J. Francis, eds, *A Reader on Preaching*. Farnham: Ashgate.

Fred Craddock, 1985. *Preaching*. Nashville, Tennessee: Abingdon Press, Chapter 9: 'The formation of the sermon'.

Fred Craddock, 2001. *As One Without Authority*, 4th edition. Atlanta, Georgia: Chalice Press.

David Day, 1998. *A Preaching Workbook*. London: SPCK, Chapter 7: 'The shapely sermon'.

David Day, 2005. 'Preaching the epistles', in David Day, Jeff Astley and Leslie J. Francis, eds, *A Reader on Preaching*. Farnham: Ashgate.

Joel Green, 2003. 'The (re-)turn to narrative', in Joel B. Green and Michael Pasquarello III, eds, *Narrative Reading, Narrative Preaching*. Ada, Mississippi: Baker Books.

Eugene Lowry, 1997. *The Sermon: Dancing the Edge of Mystery*. Nashville, Tennessee: Abingdon Press, Chapter 1: 'Time – place'.

Peter K. Stevenson, 2005. 'Preaching and narrative', in David Day, Jeff Astley and Leslie J. Francis, eds, *A Reader on Preaching*. Farnham: Ashgate.

Leonora Tubbs Tisdale, 1997. *Preaching as Local Theology and Folk Art*. Minneapolis, Minnesota: Fortress Press, Chapter 5: 'Preaching as folk art'.

Using visual images

The first two vital ingredients in any sermon are the message and the structure, deciding what God is calling you to say and planning how you want to say it. The third ingredient provides the vital spark that makes a sermon arresting and memorable. It consists of the visual images you choose to convey your message.

By 'visual images' I do not mean the use of pictures on a screen, even in these days of data projection when the internet provides such a vast array of possibilities. Rather, I mean the pictures we paint with words, through which we bring the sermon to life. Although pictures on a screen have their value, a well-chosen image, conveyed in words, is capable of conveying much more and making a much deeper and longer-lasting impact on the hearer. This is because, whereas a picture on a screen provides a ready-made image that does all the work for the observer, an image described in words asks the hearer to co-operate with the preacher. It provides an outline and leaves the hearer to fill in the details herself. And in filling in those details, she makes connections with other areas of her life experience.

Visual images in the Bible

Jesus was a master of the concrete visual image. In John's Gospel there are seven 'I am' sayings, in which Jesus provides an image through which to challenge his listeners to recognize his significance. In John 6, he says, 'I am the bread of life.' This concrete image points to a wide range of meanings and sets up a whole series of connections:

- It is connected to the miracle he had performed on the previous day, in which he provided 'enough and to spare' for everyone present.
- Bread was and is a source of life and strength.
- Bread was completely familiar in Jesus' culture, as it is in ours. In Jesus' culture there were associations with the characteristic work of the woman of the house, providing food for her family. In our own, bread is a basic commodity found in any supermarket, but there are still the resonances associated with the smell of the fresh bread counter or the bread-maker at home.
- For Jesus' original audience, the idea of Jesus providing daily bread had strong resonances with the story of the manna in the wilderness, as the dispute surrounding Jesus' saying demonstrates.

A second familiar image is that of the 'good shepherd' in John 10. This image is a bit further removed from our own culture since, except in rural areas, sheep farming is no longer familiar, and even in a community familiar with sheep the methods of the shepherd are different. But the image retains a range of meanings and connections:

- It evokes a sense of pastoral care and reliability.
- It speaks of guidance and provision.
- For Jesus' audience the image of the shepherd conjured up their memories of King David, who was 'taken from following the sheep' to be a shepherd of Israel.
- It would have brought to mind several passages in the prophets in which God promises to provide a new shepherd and others in which he himself is likened to a shepherd.

So why doesn't Jesus just say all those things? Why use the visual image at all? Because concrete images like bread and the shepherd are evocative: they don't tie down the imaginations of his hearers but invite them to make connections of their own, connections which served to anchor Jesus' teaching in their everyday life experience, teaching which they would not only remember but go on to ponder.

In using concrete visual images to speak of God and himself, Jesus is thoroughly in keeping with the Bible as a whole. In biblical terms, God is presented by means of a vast array of images. He is like 'a father, a husband, a king, a lover, a bridegroom, a warrior, a master, a vineyard owner, a lord, a consuming fire, a redeemer of a slave, a saviour, a never-failing stream, a rock, a fortress, a lion, a bear robbed of her cubs, a moth, a fountain of living water, a way, a light, bread from heaven, a shield, a potter, a mother, a sword-wielder, an axe-wielder, a judge, a plaintiff, a witness in court ...'

If we want to know what sin is like, we are presented with a similarly wide range of images. Sin is like 'becoming a harlot when one is married, or rebelling against a father's love and leaving home, or attempting to storm heaven, or forgetting the past, or wandering away like sheep, or becoming a subversive in a nation, or not being dressed when one is supposed to be ready for a wedding, or becoming like a rotten bunch of grapes in a well-tended vineyard, or trying to drink from an empty cistern when an ever-flowing stream is nearby, or breaking into a house by stealth, or leaning against a feeble reed, or making empty promises, or failing to release a neighbour from a debt ...' These lists are taken from Elizabeth Achtemeier's book, *Creative Preaching* (1980).

Theology and concrete images

The definition of an expert in a particular field is someone for whom all the jargon makes sense, who is able to think abstractly about that field. People who are not experts in that field, even highly intelligent people, tend to think about it not in abstract but in concrete terms. Thus our congregations may include highly intelligent lawyers, capable of relating particular provisions to abstract principles and discerning fine degrees of legal distinction between different situations, or business people capable of making detailed comparisons between the profitability of a variety of situations, who nevertheless still think in predominantly concrete terms when it comes to their Christian faith.

The problem for preachers who are theologically trained is that of making the journey back to the concrete ways in which we characteristically thought and spoke about our faith before our theological training *without* losing the benefits that training has given us. We may be aware, when reading a particular passage of Scripture, that the theological issue at stake concerns salvation, or incarnation, or divine justice or the call to adopt an attitude of expectant waiting, or the challenge to exercise a particular virtue like humility. Our ability to interpret the Bible in this way is our gift to our congregations. But *communicating* these abstract doctrines or principles to people without our level of theological training requires us to use concrete imagery. Perhaps that is one reason why people are so drawn to the passage in 1 Corinthians 13 in which Paul spells out what love looks like in concrete terms: patient, kind, not envious, arrogant or boastful, not insisting on its own way, keeping no score of wrongs, and so on.

Using visual images

Here are two examples of the use of imagery in sermons:

Paul Chamberlain is preaching in Advent about the need to watch and wait. He chooses an image which provides a concrete example of the idea of focusing, and then goes on to apply this to the call to focus on Jesus:

A few months ago I bought a new digital camera. It's a much better camera than the one we used to have, and I really like it. If you know anything about digital cameras, it's 12 megapixels, which means the images it takes are massive, far bigger than you would ever reasonably need.

But you know what, it's a great camera, and it ought to be for the price I paid for it – but sometimes it takes photos which are completely out of focus.

Do you know someone who just can't take good photos? Maybe there's someone in your family who just can't take pictures using a camera. In my family, it's . . . – when she takes photos they're often out of focus, or you only get the top of people's heads in, or both! That's because when she presses the button to take the picture, she also moves the whole camera. Running joke that . . . can't take pictures . . .

> That's not my problem, my problem is that the camera sometimes just doesn't focus properly! And the photos you get just look wrong. You can sort of tell what it was that the picture is of or who is in the photo, but it's blurred and you can't tell if people are smiling or angry or just bored waiting for you to take the picture . . .
>
> The picture is wrong because the focus is wrong.
>
> I think that's why we need to be watching for Jesus. Our whole picture of life will be blurred if we're not keeping our focus on the right things. Our perspective will be wrong because our focus is wrong.
>
> Life just won't look right to us. It won't look like it's meant to look. And that's why we're thinking about watching for Jesus today. Because we need to get our focus right.

Emma Pennington is preaching to theological students at the beginning of their training. She chooses the image of the road, and illustrates it from the well-known story, *The Lord of the Rings*:

> Bilbo often used to say that there was only one road; that it was like a great river: its springs were at every doorstep, and every path was its tributary. It's a dangerous thing, Frodo, going out of your door, he used to say. 'You step into the Road, and if you don't keep your feet, there is no knowing where you might be swept off to.'
>
> So says Frodo Baggins as he and Sam begin their adventures in Tolkien's *The Fellowship of the Ring*, and whether you have realized it yet or not, we have all embarked upon a new and exciting adventure. For some of you this will feel very real and raw, as you have literally stepped out into the road and left homes and jobs to be here and may be wondering where indeed you have been swept off to. For others, this is a staging post, the last homely house before the wilds of ministry. And for others it is the Shire, home with its leafy lanes and sunlit fields.

Both Paul and Emma provide vivid images, with several layers of resonance for members of their congregations, to bring alive the ideas they want to put over: the need to 'focus' on Jesus as the key to watching and waiting; and the challenges and mixed feelings surrounding the start of a new stage in life.

On one occasion I was the guest preacher at a service for Pentecost. I wanted to focus on the way the people who heard Peter preach in Acts 2 had been drawn together for the festival and were soon to go back to the many parts of the world from which they came. I wanted to make the connection between the rhythm of Christian life, in which we come together as gathered congregations each week and after worshipping together return to our daily lives, where we are called to live as disciples and witnesses for Christ. The sermon felt rather dry and 'academic' until I hit on the image of a heartbeat, through which the heart draws in blood and pumps it around the whole body, keeping us alive and healthy. The reaction from members of the congregation afterwards suggested that it was this image that had caught their attention and helped them to make sense of what I wanted to convey.

In his enthronement sermon Archbishop Rowan Williams spoke of God as a conservationist in an art gallery, patiently working away at a picture to remove the grime, oil and dust and 'let us appear in our true colours'. Another image of the way God wants to restore us and make us holy is used in the course 'Saints Alive'. It is the image of a beautiful cottage now derelict and in need of restoration. The cottage is bought by an experienced master builder, who knows exactly how to restore the cottage. Some of the jobs he has to carry out are obvious, like the removal of rotten floors. Others would only be noticed by other experts, but are just as essential. The builder has an image in his mind of what the cottage will look like when restoration is complete and does not give up until he has finished the job. A third image for this same process, our growth in holiness through the work of the Holy Spirit, might be that of an experienced surgeon treating a patient with a complicated condition. The surgeon knows the right order in which a series of operations needs to be undertaken, and is content to give the patient time for rest and recovery between each one.

In each of these examples, the preacher is doing what Jesus did so often: taking an example from daily life and using it as an image to illustrate a spiritual principle. But the most productive source of concrete visual pictures for preaching is likely to be the Bible itself. As we have seen, biblical language tends to be concrete. Jesus points us to the 'lilies of the field', to the outcome of seed sown in a variety of different soils. He uses the action of yeast, the experience of finding buried treasure, the process of fishermen sorting their catch and a vast array of other images to evoke a sense of what God's kingdom is all about. And of course, his parables provide more images for God, and his relationship with and his expectations of his people.

But Jesus is not the only image-maker in the New Testament. The epistles abound in them. In the space of a few verses in 1 Thessalonians 5, Paul gives us a thief breaking into a house at night, the onset of labour pains, darkness and light, night and day, sleeping and waking, drunkenness and sobriety, a breastplate, a helmet and finally the image of 'building one another up'.

Alvin Rueter points to the image of the bride in Ephesians 5. Only this bride is dressed in dirty clothes. 'What a picture that made when I described a wedding where by tradition everybody else marches to the altar with every eyelash in place and standing at attention waiting for the bride to enter – and here she comes, reeking with mothballs, her hair stringy and dishevelled, her dress blotched with gravy and beer. That led me to find a lot of pictures of what our Lord has to put up with in forgiving and sanctifying the Church' (1997, p. 70).

Rueter's example, like those from Paul Chamberlain and Emma Pennington, shows us that using visual imagery involves more than simply *mentioning* the image. Using visual imagery well involves painting a picture, drawing the congregation into the image, enabling them to feel the feelings, smell the smells, giving them a sense of what is at stake. In this way the preacher creates a vivid concrete picture, easy to understand and remember, to convey the meaning of an abstract principle: the cost to Jesus of 'forgiving and sanctifying the Church', the commitment required in responding to God's call, the requirement of 'focus' as an element in Advent waiting.

And sometimes a biblical image or theme requires a modern-day image for clarity. The writer to the Hebrews writes of approaching God 'with our hearts sprinkled clean from an evil conscience', using an image which would have made perfect sense to his readers, familiar with the rites of the Jewish sacrificial system. I puzzled as to how to convey this in an up-to-date way until I remembered looking inside the engine of my car just after it had been steam-cleaned so as to detect whether there was an oil leak. David Day writes of one preacher seeking to convey the sense of 'seeking first the kingdom of God': single-minded, concentrating on only one thing, like an Olympic rifle-shooter, eye, hand, finger, arms, stance, even breathing, focused on the target; and taking no notice at all of the sound of the spectators, a loudspeaker announcement far away, the need to get the car serviced, what he will eat for dinner tonight, and so on (2005, pp. 66–7). In fact, Day's book takes this whole area much further with a wide-ranging examination of how we can 'embody' the word by the use of concrete images.

Illustrations

Illustrations are images that 'move': images that have now developed to become stories. Like images, they embody the message of the sermon in a concrete way, but do this by means of a fully fledged story, with a beginning, middle and end.

Illustrations are the preacher's bread and butter. Almost every book on preaching (and this one is no exception) assumes that preachers will use illustrations, stories from life which flesh out the point the preacher wants to make by showing how it might work out in practice.

But using illustrations is not without its problems. Writing in 1998 in *A Preaching Workbook*, David Day majored on the things that can go wrong with inappropriate illustrations. In *Embodying the Word* in 2005 he is much more positive: an illustration may be an 'unexploded bomb' but that doesn't mean it should be left for the bomb disposal squad!

The huge advantage of illustrations is that they make the point concrete: they show us someone acting on the principle we intend to teach, an actual example of someone rising to a challenge. They help offer inspiration by sketching a picture of what might be. They can be used to gain interest, to amuse, as a way of identifying with the congregation or giving the sermon credibility.

But illustrations also have their drawbacks. Used wrongly they can effectively sabotage the sermon, leaving people confused and even angry. Here are some of the commonest pitfalls:

- The illustration is too powerful. The emotions it evokes are so strong that they 'leak' into the rest of the sermon, distracting the hearers' attention from the message the preacher wants to convey.
- The illustration carries a lot of cultural baggage. It may give the impression the preacher is out of touch with the world of the congregation or may even disparage the congregation's culture.
- The illustration actually confuses the issue. It is a good story but it doesn't really illustrate the point the preacher wants to make. Or it does illustrate it, and several other points as well.
- The preacher uses the illustration in a way that is too prescriptive: he says, in effect, 'Now everyone should put the message of the sermon

into practice in this way.' Any particular example can only be one way of putting the message into practice, so we need to be careful not to leave people thinking we have told them precisely what to do.

- The illustrative story you want to use has the wrong intention: your intention was to encourage but you use a challenging story in your conclusion.

Stories are open-ended. They invite the listener to make multiple connections from his or her own experience. Unless you make it clear *what* the story is intended to illustrate, it is very possible that your listeners will take away a different application from the one you intended. Not only that, but the story is usually very much more memorable than the principle it is intended to illustrate, with the result that people may easily go away remembering the story but forgetting the principle.

In terms of the learning cycle that we looked at in Chapter 2, illustrations are the action phase of the cycle: they show a principle actually being put into practice. Their usefulness lies in the fact that ready-made concepts are not easily absorbed. The illustration helps to show the concept in concrete form. But the learning cycle also shows that action leads to experience and then analysis or reflection. In other words, on hearing a story, the way people are most likely to respond is to think about what it would have been like to be the person in the story and make connections with their own experience, leading to their own conclusions. The reason that people so often remember only the story is that we don't give them time to work through the cycle and we fail to use the cycle to guide them back to the principle we intended to teach.

So unless we are careful an illustration can lead the listeners away from the conclusion we are hoping for rather than reinforce it. The rule then is to tie the story or example securely into the principle you intend it to illustrate. State the principle – tell the story – and then *restate* the principle. Or even better, having told the story, add your own reflection which leads back to the principle.

In my outline sermon on the parable of the sower I suggested that a major element in the conclusion might be a story that illustrates either good or bad listening, preferably good listening. If you were to use a story in this way it would be important to begin by stating the principle it is designed to reinforce: 'Good listening can be life-giving', or even the message of the sermon itself, 'The way you listen determines the way you live.' Having told the story, it would then be helpful to pause and allow the congregation to reflect on the outcome, perhaps with the use of a phrase designed to encourage reflection such as, 'I wonder how . . . felt when she knew . . . had really got the message' or 'I can only imagine the effect this must have had on their relationship.' Then, in the course of wrapping up the sermon as a whole, state the principle again so as to be sure it gets home.

EXERCISE 3E

What is Jesus telling us about himself when he uses the following images?

- The light of the world
- The door of the sheepfold
- The resurrection and the life
- The vine.

Think about both the 'everyday' resonances and the place of these images in Israel's tradition.

For each of these, what modern-day images can you think of to convey a similar range of meanings?

EXERCISE 3F

Each of the following passages uses a concrete image from daily life in New Testament times to convey something of the meaning of our salvation. See if you can discern what that image is and, where possible, suggest what a similar up-to-date image might be:

- 'For the Son of Man came not to be served but to serve, and to give his life a ransom for many' (Mark 10.45).
- 'All this is from God, who reconciled us to himself through Christ' (2 Corinthians 5.18).
- 'And forgive us our debts, as we also have forgiven our debtors' (Matthew 6.12).
- 'The kingdom of heaven may be compared to a king who gave a wedding banquet for his son . . .' (Matthew 22.2).
- 'His master said to him, "Well done, good and trustworthy slave; you have been trustworthy in a few things, I will put you in charge of many things; enter into the joy of your master"' (Matthew 25.23).
- 'He has rescued us from the power of darkness and transferred us into the kingdom of his beloved Son' (Colossians 1.13).

EXERCISE 3G

Prepare a five-minute Advent talk based on 1 Thessalonians 5.1–11.

The passage offers a variety of vivid images around which to base your talk:

- a thief in the night
- the onset of labour
- light and darkness
- drowsiness and wakefulness
- drunkenness and sobriety
- defensive armour
- 'building one another up'.

For a talk of only five minutes, it is best to choose one and stick with it.

Make sure you identify a message, intention and hoped-for outcome for your talk. In this case, the choice of message, etc., will be influenced by the image that you find most striking. But it is important not to confuse the message with the image you are going to use to convey it.

The image will be the main body of your talk. Think about how you will convey it as vividly as possible. Don't forget to suggest the feelings that might be evoked.

References

Elizabeth Achtemeier, 1980. *Creative Preaching.* Nashville, Tennessee: Abingdon Press.

J. R. R. Tolkien, 1954. *The Fellowship of the Ring.* London: George Allen and Unwin.

Further reading

Fred Craddock, 1985. *Preaching.* Nashville, Tennessee: Abingdon Press, Chapter 10: 'Enriching the form'.

David Day, 1998. *A Preaching Workbook.* London: SPCK, Chapter 6: 'Learning from the experts'; Chapter 9: 'The eggstain on the waistcoat'; Chapter 10: 'A funny thing happened to me . . .'

David Day, 2005. *Embodying the Word.* London: SPCK.

Richard L. Eslinger, 2005. 'Story and image in sermon illustration', in David Day, Jeff Astley and Leslie J. Francis, eds, *A Reader on Preaching.* Farnham: Ashgate.

Jolyon Mitchell, 2005. 'Preaching pictures', in David Day, Jeff Astley and Leslie J. Francis, eds, *A Reader on Preaching.* Farnham: Ashgate.

Alvin C. Rueter, 1997. *Making Good Preaching Better*. Collegeville, Minnesota: Liturgical Press, Chapter 6: 'Making homilies visual'.

Thomas H. Troeger, 1990. *Imagining a Sermon*. Nashville, Tennessee: Abingdon Press.

Language to listen to

A sermon is a spoken event. The 'sermon' is not the script, even where that script is available to take away and read, but the event in which the sermon is delivered and the congregation responds. That event takes place only once; its impact must therefore be immediate. The congregation has one chance to hear the message – even where it is available afterwards through the internet, the immediate impact needs to be sufficient to persuade them to listen again – so the sermon must be as comprehensible as possible at first hearing.

The preacher has at her disposal the range of the spoken voice, tone and expression, pace and pauses, as well as bodily gestures, through which to convey her meaning. Important as they are, I have chosen not to address them in this book because I am not an expert. The best short introduction I know is Geoffrey Stevenson's chapter, 'The act of delivery' in *Preaching with Humanity* (Stevenson and Wright, 2008). But the best ways to learn delivery are to record oneself – using video where possible – and listen or watch oneself; and to receive feedback from others. What one can address at the stage of preparation is the choice of words and phrasing.

The language of the sermon needs to be spoken language – language to listen to. A common complaint is that the preacher has 'read' his sermon. This may mean that he was tied to the script, rarely making eye contact with the congregation. Often, however, it means that he used the language of the written rather than the spoken word. The sermon came across as an essay, which might have been addressed to anyone, rather than a message designed to be delivered to a particular congregation at a particular time and place.

In this section we will try to tease out the difference between written and spoken language. This is not straightforward, for several reasons:

- first, because in several respects the difference is one of degree;
- second, because the style of spoken language differs considerably from place to place and from culture to culture;

- third, because on many occasions and for many congregations the language of the sermon, while remaining the language of speech, needs to be slightly more formal than the language of *everyday* speech.

Getting the register just right for a particular congregation usually comes gradually and reflects the preacher's personality and the relationship between her and the congregation. But it is possible to suggest some guidelines. First, compare extracts A and B in the following two examples, which are about the parables of the dishonest steward and the lost sheep. In each case extract A is intended as an example of written language, extract B an example of spoken language. What differences can you discern between them?

A

Among the parables of Jesus this is perhaps one of the most difficult to interpret. Although there is considerable uncertainty over its application to our situation, the issue appears to revolve around the use of money. Underlying the case of the manager, whose job was the handling of his master's money, is the assumption that God is both creator and redeemer, whose ownership of the world requires that what we are used to thinking of as our own belongs by right to him. Rather than commending the manager's dishonesty, what impressed the master would seem to have been his shrewdness. This being so, the challenge lies in the area of personal finance: whether each Christian knows sufficiently well how God expects his or her money to be used and whether he or she is skilled in so doing.

B

Many of the parables include a surprise and this is one of the most puzzling of all. Is Jesus really teaching us to be like the dishonest manager, who used his master's money to feather his own nest? Let's take the parable step by step.

First, the parable is about a steward: a man whose job was to manage his master's money. How does that apply to us? We are used to thinking of the money we earn and the things we buy with it as our own. But is that really the case? Who is it who really provides all the good things of this world? Is it not God, who created the world that we enjoy? And not only does our money belong to God because he created it. It also belongs to him because we belong to him. We have been 'bought with a price', and everything we have is his.

Second, the man in the story was dishonest, but he was also shrewd. Handling money was his bread and butter and in a tight corner he knew what to do. He set out to make friends for himself by swindling his master. The master also knew a thing or two about finance. He knew the manager was dishonest. Now he realized he was also very astute.

So what is the point that Jesus is making in this parable? I wonder if it is this: are you using your money in the way God expects? When it comes to handling money, are you as skilled at using it to build for God's kingdom as the manager was in looking after himself?

A

In general, the degree of gratitude one feels is dependent on the perception of the favour received. Towards the person who has performed a small favour, we may feel mildly grateful, whereas a much keener sense of obligation can be expected towards a person who has saved our life.

The parable of the good shepherd suggests that our case is closer to the latter than to the former. At great cost to himself, Jesus has carried out a rescue. He came, like the shepherd, to search for those who were lost. The challenge is how our obligation towards him is most appropriately expressed.

B

Suppose I happen to meet you in the street and offer you a chocolate. You'd probably think I was a generous and friendly person. You'd smile when you saw me again. Perhaps if the opportunity came around you'd offer me a sweet in return.

But now, suppose that one day you accidentally step out in front of a bus, and I jump out and grab you and pull you to safety just in time. I wonder how you'd feel about me then. I expect you'd be amazingly grateful, ready to do anything you could for me.

Many Christians make the mistake of thinking that what Jesus has done for us is like giving us a chocolate. Our life was basically fine, and Jesus has made it a little bit better. And so we're mildly grateful.

> We're pleased to be Christians and come to church, but that's as far as it goes.
>
> But according to the story of the lost sheep that is very far from the truth. In fact, we were lost. We were in a mess and things were only likely to get worse. But Jesus has come to the rescue. He came looking for us, at amazing cost, and went on searching until he found us. How then do we express our gratitude?

There are several differences between the two extracts in each of these examples:

- In both cases extract A is more distant and impersonal. The first refers to 'each Christian' and uses 'he or she', 'him or her'; the second uses the pronoun 'one'. They are written for an unknown audience, to be read in a wide variety of circumstances. The use of 'the former' and 'the latter' in the second example depends on the reader's ability to check back to remind himself which the former and the latter situations were. In contrast, in extract B I refer to 'I', 'you' and 'us'. It is meant to be spoken in the context of the relationship between preacher and congregation.
- The sense of distance in the two A extracts is further heightened by the use of formal phrases to express uncertainty: 'the issue seems to be', 'appears to revolve around' and 'would seem to have been'. In the B extracts I have not avoided uncertainty but approached it in a more direct way: 'I wonder if it's this.'
- The A extracts are marked by the use of abstract concepts: 'obligation', 'the handling of', 'creator and redeemer'. In the B extracts I make use of these abstract concepts but in each case I try to unpack them. I create a concrete example to explain the contrast between a relatively mild and a much stronger sense of obligation. I spell out (if only briefly) what it means to believe in God as creator and redeemer. And in the parable of the dishonest manager 'the handling of' becomes 'to handle': an activity rather than an abstract concept.
- Because reading is fast, sentence order can be relatively complex in order to express nuances of meaning. The sentence in A beginning 'Underlying the case of the manager' includes a number of separate clauses, making a comparison between the manager's position

and ours under God. In extract B I have used nine sentences to express the meaning conveyed by this one sentence in A. Not only are these sentences shorter but they are intended to build gradually. Because the sermon is spoken communication, it is also possible, and sometimes advisable, to use repetition in order to give the listeners a second chance to grasp a more difficult concept, something which can become tedious on paper.

- The outcome of this is that spoken language has far fewer subordinate clauses and 'twisty' sentences than written language. Spoken language also has far more short sentences. Sometimes a series of short sentences provide short steps, enabling the hearers to follow the argument. Sometimes they heighten the tension: 'In fact, we were lost. We were in a mess and things were only likely to get worse. But Jesus has come to the rescue.' In fact, spoken language can be understood without the use of complete sentences. Without becoming sloppy, it is possible to stretch the rules of grammar to increase impact and clarity.

- Not only do the B extracts include many more short sentences, but many of these are also rhetorical questions. The rhetorical question is a characteristic feature of spoken language, much rarer in written language. I hope that the examples I have given are not overloaded with questions because we must be careful not to overdo them. But they express and build on the relationship between preacher and congregation and the immediacy of the situation.

- Finally, in all cases I have removed the passives from the A extracts. 'Can be expected' becomes 'I expect' and 'is most appropriately expressed', 'How then do we express . . . ?' Almost always, the passive mood is more distant and impersonal than the active.

As well as these contrasts in construction, there are some distinctive features of the vocabulary in the B extracts:

- They include idiomatic phrases such as 'feather his own nest', 'bread and butter', 'knew a thing or two' and 'tight corner'. Choosing the right vocabulary depends a great deal on the audience. As a public speaker, your vocabulary and phrasing may be a little more formal than your congregation's usual style of conversational speech, but it should not be so much more formal as to make it difficult for them to understand.

- Abbreviations such as 'let's', 'I'd' and 'you'd' are generally acceptable in spoken language but not in written language.
- Although I want the congregation to understand the vocabulary I choose, I don't want to limit it. I will still try to choose the most evocative words possible. In these extracts I have used 'surprising' and 'puzzling' in place of 'difficult to interpret'; and I have used a variety of evocative words for the manager's ability: 'shrewd', 'astute' and 'skilled'.
- On the other hand I have tried to avoid 'stuffy' language. Phrases like 'degree of gratitude' and 'appears to revolve' have been rewritten. In sermons, people don't 'proceed', they 'go'; or, more evocatively, 'travel', or if the context allows it, they may 'hurry' or even 'trek'.

In both cases the versions designed to be spoken are longer than the versions in written language. This is because of the need to unpack some abstract concepts and disentangle one or two involved sentences. Usually, spoken communication will be longer than written, but this is not always the case, especially when excess verbiage is a feature of a particular writer's written style.

Look at the following extracts, first from Julia Baldwin, second from Tom Carson, and take note of as many features as possible of *spoken* language. Note also that Tom's intended outcome is a definite action. We will see how this is reflected in his conclusion in a later section.

Message: The Lord is your Shepherd – no matter what – trust in him.
Intention: Illustrate how God moves in the pain and darkness of our lives.
Outcome: New perspective of God's action in the midst of our pain and darkness.

The Lord is my Shepherd. He certainly is. I don't know about you but Psalm 23 is one of my favourites; one of those Bible passages that comes to hand in times of crisis and celebration – a psalm for all seasons – a comfort when it feels like we're walking down the *valley of the shadow of death* and a celebration psalm when we sense God up close in our lives. For me it sums up the Christian journey: who God is and who we are in relation to him. He is the shepherd, we are the sheep. And sometimes it's good to be reminded of that.

He has led us, he is leading us now and will lead us into the future – Psalm 23 gives us confidence in a God who is *active* in our lives – not just a passive companion walking alongside – he directs us (with his staff), he gives us rest and refreshment (by still waters), he defends us (with his rod), feeds us (in green pastures) and invites us into his home . . .

Message: Jesus is coming – make space for him.
Intention: Inspire to spirituality.
Outcome: They will make more space for God in their lives during Advent, perhaps practically through using a tea-light to pray.

Introduction

'Jesus is coming – look busy'. So says the amusing print on the front of many T-shirts you may have seen. As though busy-ness will somehow make it look like we're living the kind of lives we ought to be.

After all, *busy-ness* is something we're pretty good at. Our diaries get full of meetings, social events, and to-do lists . . . Even among the retired, I've often heard the comment, 'I don't know how I used to have the time for work!' We can easily sympathize with Basil Fawlty: *Zoom! What was that? That was your life, Mate! That was quick, do I get another? Sorry, Mate.* There are, of course, times when we get ourselves so busy that we forget ourselves in the midst of it. One philosopher put it like this . . .

> By seeing the multitude of people around, by being busied with all sorts of worldly affairs, by being wise in the ways of the world, sometimes a person forgets themselves . . . finds it much easier and safer to be like the others, to become a copy, a number, along with the crowd. Precisely by losing himself in this way, such a person gains all that is required for a flawless performance in everyday life, yes, for making a great success out of life . . .

This piece of writing by Kierkegaard, who lived over 150 years ago, could describe many people's lives today. In our busy-ness we can forget who we are created to be – and simply live in conformity to the world around. Never is this more true than in the run-up to

Christmas, the season in which there is so much to be done to get ourselves ready.

This run-up begins today on the first Sunday of Advent. Like the T-shirt, Advent is a reminder to us that Jesus is coming . . . But I'm not sure that looking busy is quite the right response. And so as we reflect this morning on Christ's coming, let's hold in our mind's eyes all the things we'll be doing in the four weeks ahead and how we might best prepare for him.

Using notes

Congregations object when the preacher reads his sermon. In many cases this is because the sermon is in written style. It sounds like a piece of writing, not like something designed to be spoken. But there is also a deeper issue. Congregations expect the message to be authentic: they expect the preacher to be preaching from the heart. How can he be doing this if he has to read his sermon? How can the congregation be expected to remember it if he can't remember it himself without referring to his notes?

Does this mean that we should therefore try to do without notes? Most of the great preachers of the past have counselled against this. Many have preached from a full script – although the script will be written as *spoken* rather than written language. I suggest that this difference between spoken and written language, rather than the kind of notes we use, answers the first objection: sermons that sound more like essays. Attention to the structure of the sermon will help you to remember it better: you will have a sense of how you want it to flow from point to point. And the better you can remember it the more independent you will be of your notes. You might try to memorize each sermon as well as possible so as to rely on notes even less, but this will not guarantee that the sermon comes from your heart. The only way to answer that objection is to let the Scripture passage and the message you choose speak as powerfully to you as you want them to speak to the congregation. The key is this: don't 'write' your sermons, 'prepare' them – and yourself – for delivery.

Nevertheless, it is important to use a style of notes that helps you to engage with the congregation: to make regular eye contact and to be intuitively aware of their response as you preach. However you make notes, it is important that the paper be a convenient size either for holding in your hand or placing on the reading desk; that the font (or the writing) should be large enough to be read easily; and that you develop a consistent notation for reminding yourself to pause or slow down at particular passages; possibly even to remind yourself of the gestures you intend to make at particular points: 'smile here' or 'raise right hand', 'raise left hand'.

In an earlier section I included the notes for a sermon on the parable of the sower as a mind-map. I find this useful because it enables me to fit the whole sermon on to one piece of paper. It provides an overview of the structure and a sense of how far through the sermon I am at any given point. It also enables me to miss bits out or even change the order of a sermon in mid-flow if either should prove necessary.

However, it is difficult to include more than outline notes when using a mind-map and I tend to use this form of notes only when I am reasonably confident. On occasions when I know I am likely to be nervous and on all occasions when it is important to stick closely to a prepared script I use a form of notes close to, though not exactly the same as, a full script. I have adapted this method from the American preacher Peter Marshall.

The particular sermon is one I wrote for a wedding based on the film *Notting Hill*. The film is a bit too old now for the sermon to be usable. See Figure 3.3.

EXERCISE 3H

Look back at some of your previous sermons. Look for examples of passages that are in written rather than spoken English and see how you could improve them. For example:

- Shorten any overlong sentences.
- Straighten out any twisted sentences or groups of sentences, i.e. remove any subordinate clause, build the idea in the way people can grasp it best.
- Replace passive expressions with active ones.
- Change any words or expressions that are too wordy and say it more simply.
- Change or remove abstract nouns and unnecessary qualifying adjectives.

Paper size: A5
Font: Arial Bold 10 point
Tab settings: every 0.5 cm

Notting Hill wedding sermon

Message: commitment is a God-given dream
Intention: teach and inspire
Outcome: recognize commitment as heart of marriage

In the film Notting Hill
scene with Hugh Grant and Julia Roberts
together at night, in a communal garden, middle London square
they come upon a bench, inscribed with the words
for June who loved this garden,
from Joseph who always sat beside her
Julia Roberts looks at it and says
some people do spend their whole lives together

She's come from the world of Hollywood
relationships seem to be glitz and glamour, but only on the surface
looking for something deeper
genuine love that will last for ever
She's expressing the longing that most of us have for permanence
relationship that will be like that garden
a protected space in the midst of surrounding world
and one that will last a lifetime

Problem: we don't really know how to get it
it remains there as ideal that we haven't given up on
but we don't know whether our lives will ever attain that ideal

Answer to that longing is here today in the words of the wedding service,
words that N and M are saying to one another, and all that they mean

---

Set out message, intention and outcome at the top to remind you as you pray before preaching.

In general, one item of meaning on each line.

Use part sentences or short phrases.

Useful for thinking about the best choice of words.

Omit unimportant words.

Signal where you want to leave a pause.

Figure 3.3

EXERCISE 3I

In Romans 1.1–7 Paul is introducing himself and his message to a group of people he has not yet met. Suppose he had got to Rome before his letter arrived. What would he have said?

Rewrite Romans 1.1–7 in *spoken* English.

Further reading

Charles Chadwick and Phillip Tovey, 2001. *Developing Reflective Practice for Preachers*, Grove W164. Cambridge: Grove.

Fred Craddock, 1985. *Preaching*. Nashville, Tennessee: Abingdon Press, Chapter 10: 'Enriching the form'.

David Day, 1998. *A Preaching Workbook*. London: SPCK, Chapter 8: 'Faith, hope and clarity'.

Alvin Rueter, 1997. *Making Good Preaching Better*. Collegeville, Minnesota: Liturgical Press, Chapter 7: 'Making homilies oral'.

Andy Stanley and Lane Jones, 2006. *Communicating for a Change*. Colorado Springs, Colorado: Multnomah Press, Chapter 14: 'Internalize the message'.

Geoffrey Stevenson, 2008. 'The act of delivery', in Geoffrey Stevenson and Stephen I. Wright, eds, *Preaching with Humanity*. London: Church House Publishing.

Thomas H. Troeger, 1990. *Imagining a Sermon*. Nashville, Tennessee: Abingdon Press, Chapter 4: 'Listen to the music of speech'.

Getting started

You have perhaps two minutes, seldom more, to persuade your congregation to listen to you! Listening takes an effort. The world is full of information, most of which we know from experience that we cannot make use of, so we become used to filtering it out, remembering only what we think we need to know. To listen to a connected discourse takes concentration; to listen to one that we know may challenge us, perhaps even ask us to change our ways, requires not only effort but commitment. Is it surprising that so many regular churchgoers, however well-intentioned they may be, find their attention drifting during a sermon? You have two minutes to persuade them to make the effort, to convince them that the sermon you have worked hard to prepare will be worth listening to.

So your introduction must grab people's attention. It must point forward to the rest of the sermon, letting them know what is coming, providing clear directions to help them to listen. On the other hand, it must avoid gimmicks. The preacher who began his sermon by riding a bicycle down the central aisle was remembered long afterwards – but no one could recall what the sermon had actually been about! A joke may help the congregation relax and raise anticipation of further entertainment to come, but unless it has something to do with the message of the sermon as a whole it is more likely to be a distraction. Humour is a great gift, but it is best deployed gently woven into the text rather than simply as an attention-grabber.

An introduction has four elements, each of which, without the aid of gimmicks, helps a congregation to concentrate and whets their appetite for what is to come. The extent to which you will actually deploy each one will depend on circumstances, your knowledge of the particular congregation and the message you want to convey. Here they are:

Element 1: Establish rapport

A sermon takes place in the context of a relationship between preacher and congregation. If you are a guest preacher or relatively unknown, you will need to introduce yourself, not in a formal way but by giving enough personal information to establish a rapport. Some remarks about the occasion and what it means to you may be enough.

If you are well known, it may not be necessary to say anything by way of introduction. But there is a deeper level of rapport which may be extremely important. This turns on what the message you are preaching means to you. How do the truths about God you want to convey affect you personally? If your message is an encouragement, how does it encourage you? If it is a challenge, how do you respond to the challenge and, perhaps, where do you fall short? You may be the preacher but you are also a disciple like the members of the congregation, and as disciples we are all in this together. Your audience will want what you are telling them to carry a note of authenticity, so it is vital to establish rapport.

Element 2: State the theme of the sermon

What is the sermon going to be about? Unless they know this within the first few minutes it is almost certain that the congregation will switch off. In fact, I would say that this is one of the most frequent preaching mistakes. Too many preachers leave their audience in suspense: they spend too long on a striking story or personal anecdote and fail to let them know what the subject of the sermon is to be. Not knowing this, the congregation rapidly loses concentration.

It is not always necessary to state the message at the beginning of the sermon, especially when you are using an inductive structure, which saves the statement of the message until nearer to the end. The congregation needs to know what you are going to talk about but not necessarily what you are going to say about it. Which of the Scripture passages they have just heard read to them are you going to talk about? What aspect are you going to concentrate on? Is there a question you are going to answer? If the sermon is inductive, what area of experience are you going to ask them to consider? If it is narrative, what is the subject of the story you are about to tell? Don't expect your audience to be able to work this out for themselves – tell them clearly.

Element 3: Why should they want to listen to this?

It is an axiom of adult education, amply confirmed by research, that adults learn best when they can see that the subject is relevant to them. And for both adults and children, good practice in education is to allow the learners to know what the objectives of the teaching session are. To tell your congregation why you think the sermon might be important to them is neither spoon-feeding nor coercion. They remain free to disagree with you and disengage at any stage. It is a way of inviting them to co-operate with you, and the person who wants to learn and can see the point is much more likely to retain what you hope to teach.

So as well as stating clearly what the theme of the sermon is to be, an introduction will often include a sentence or two to suggest why this particular topic is important and what difference it might make in people's lives. If possible, it creates tension, a sense of something unresolved, an issue to be thought through, a need to know, that keeps people listening.

Element 4: How do you want them to listen?

This fourth element of an introduction is the most often omitted. It may not be necessary on every occasion, but the most common reason for omission, in my opinion, is that it is much the most difficult for us, as preachers, either to comprehend or to put into practice. So what am I actually suggesting here?

Listening is not straightforward, nor is it simply a passive exercise. Good listening is a skill and good listening to a sermon a particularly difficult skill. That is why telling your congregation what the sermon is to be about and why they might want to listen to it is so important. But there is another question: *how* do you want people to listen?

If this is to be a narrative sermon, you want the congregation to be ready to listen to a story. This is a relatively familiar activity and one that most people are good at. What they are less good at, though, is grasping the *point* of the story, which is why announcing the theme of the sermon before embarking on the story, or providing a reflection on the story after telling it, can be a great help. If you are preaching an inductive sermon, you hope that the congregation will want to engage with you in thinking deeply about a particular area of life. In which case, why not tell them that this is what you would like them to do?

Crafting a sentence in which you signal how you want people to listen is not easy. Knowing your intention and your intended outcome will help you immeasurably in working out how to do it. And this extra bit of attention to the introduction may well pay huge dividends.

Examples

It is not always necessary to include all four of these elements in an introduction. You may judge that the subject is likely to be interesting enough and there is no need to persuade the congregation to listen. The announcement of the theme may in itself make it clear how best people can listen. Circumstances, your relationship with them and the message itself will influence how much you include.

Moreover, these four elements do not always need to come at the beginning of the sermon. The impact of the subject on you personally may be better stated much later. The importance of the theme for our Christian discipleship may need to be emphasized more than once and at various points in the sermon. The mode of listening may change, perhaps from puzzling about an issue to listening to a story and back again.

For these reasons it is best to see the introduction itself as an 'element' in the sermon, along with interpretation, application and conclusion, rather than simply the part that comes at the beginning.

This allows us to be flexible in preparation, deploying the elements of the introduction itself in the best way.

Having said that, let us now look at three actual introductions: the passages from the sermons of Julia Baldwin and Tom Carson from the previous section and the introduction to my outline sermon on the parable of the sower from the section on structure.

The outline for my sermon clearly shows the four elements of the introduction and suggests how I might include each one. The intention of this sermon is to challenge, so I have chosen to begin it with a story that introduces the challenge by illustrating the consequences of failing to listen. I might follow this up with one or two incidents from my own experience, making the point that I too am not a very good listener. The stories both build rapport and suggest the importance of the theme. I then plan to say that we are going to pay attention to the way that we listen, which in itself suggests how I want the congregation to listen to this sermon. And the reason I am asking them to do this is given in the message itself: 'The way you listen determines the way you live.'

Tom announces the theme of the sermon – busy-ness – in the first sentence, and this introduces a prolonged reflection on the busy ways in which many people live their lives and the costs of this busy-ness. He does not specifically refer to himself, but he uses the words 'we' and 'our' some 14 times to make it clear that 'we' are in this together. Then at the end of the introductory section, he asks the congregation to think ahead to everything they expect to be doing in the weeks leading up to Christmas and to ask the question how best they can prepare for Christ's coming.

Julia begins by stating the message in her first sentence. She then goes on to say that Psalm 23 is a personal favourite and gives some of the reasons for that. By now it is clear that Psalm 23, and specifically the image of Jesus as the good shepherd, is to be the theme of the sermon. What she has not yet done is apply the psalm to the areas of pain and darkness in our lives. She will include this element of the introduction later, when applying the image of the shepherd to specific occasions. What she has done is to say that the sermon is to be a reminder of what God's active presence in our lives can mean. Perhaps she could make this even clearer by adding a sentence at the end of the first paragraph inviting her hearers to focus on what God's presence means to them, especially in times of pain.

Fitting the structure

The way we use the introduction will depend on the structure of the sermon. In a narrative sermon it may be preferable to begin straight in with the story and save the 'introduction' for later, the point at which you may want to draw attention to the theme, say what the story means to you, and perhaps to ask your hearers to consider what struck them. An inductive sermon differs from a deductive one precisely in that for an inductive sermon you save the announcement of the message until near the end, whereas for a deductive sermon you state the message up front. It is, nevertheless, important in an inductive sermon to make sure that your listeners know the theme.

If you are using 'problem–solution' then the sermon begins with an exploration of the problem, which may include why this is so important to us all, the impact on you personally and even how you want people to consider it, but leaving the solution – the message – until later. Similarly in 'not this . . . nor this . . . but this' you will introduce the question and perhaps ask the listeners to consider their own answer before coming to the answer you want to give.

The introduction may be very short. It may consist of no more than a question which itself indicates the theme before going straight into the body of the sermon. But it needs to be long enough to do its job: to invite people's attention by creating rapport, letting them know what the sermon is to be about, suggesting why this might be important to them and providing some indication of how you would like them to listen while you talk.

Anticipation

Anticipation is a wonderful device for preachers. Used well it can greatly help to keep people listening and get them thinking along with you. Examples of the use of anticipation might include a question that you will answer only later in the sermon; a story that you don't interpret straight away; a story that stops halfway and is finished only later or even in the conclusion. In my 'parable' sermon, which I used in the section on the varieties of structure, I told two stories, asking the congregation to finish them for themselves, before completing them as part of the conclusion.

Anticipation can also be used on a small scale to focus attention on an important point. You can pause before giving the conclusion to an illustration: 'I wonder what she replied . . . I wonder what you would have replied . . . In fact what she said was . . .' You can introduce an element of mystery to an illustration: 'When I was a child I had a favourite place that I loved to go. I didn't have far to go to find this place, but when I was there I was quite alone. My favourite place was . . .' In his famous Washington address Martin Luther King emphasized the demand for emancipation by summing it up in, 'Three little words. They're not big words. They're not complicated words. We want it *here*, we want it *all*, and we want it *now*.'

Personal disclosure

I have suggested that part of the role of an introduction is to establish rapport with the congregation and that one of the ways to do this is through personal disclosure. The wisdom or otherwise of personal disclosure is a frequently recurring subject in books on preaching and there is a considerable variety of opinion. Some writers point to the dangers of allowing the preacher's own opinions, emotions or struggles to take centre stage and urge him to avoid talking about himself. Others place the emphasis on authenticity, for which an appropriate degree of personal openness is required.

All I can do is to give my own opinion. Throughout this book I have emphasized the relationship between preacher and congregation. Each sermon both expresses and contributes to that relationship. It is important for the preacher to know and love the congregation and important that they are aware that she knows and loves them. Without such confidence it is unlikely that they will be open to listen to what she says: her encouragement will lack conviction and her challenge will go unheeded.

Preaching involves immediacy. It is about this particular person bringing a specific message to a congregation at a particular time and place. Who that person is and what the message means to her personally is therefore a major element in the message itself. For all these reasons, appropriate self-disclosure is a vital element in preaching.

And in fact self-disclosure is unavoidable. As preacher you are telling people about yourself all the time. Your tone of voice and choice of expressions themselves indicate whether or not you are confident in this particular message. The way you refer to the Bible will demonstrate whether or not you know and love it, and whether your own life is moulded by Scripture. To use a personal illustration is simply an extension of what is taking place anyway whenever you preach.

On the other hand, our task is to point to Jesus and it is vital that we do not get in the way. Personal illustration is fine as long as what it reveals is a healthy and humble relationship with the Lord and with fellow Christians. Personal disclosure should reveal us to be neither better nor worse than the congregation: fellow pilgrims who sometimes succeed through God's grace and sometimes fail. The sermon is not usually a good time to air our personal doubts and struggles unless we have come to a place of resolution and have some wisdom to share. Otherwise, as the psalmist says from his own place of struggle, we may be 'untrue to the circle of your children' (Psalm 73.15). We also need to pay attention to whether a personal illustration is actually true, whether we are presenting ourselves in a better light than may perhaps be deserved, whether the story has been subtly doctored to leave out the embarrassing bits. And even if it is true, is it helpful? Stories of success are often more discouraging than stories of failure, unless it is clear that the success was due to God's grace rather than our ability. What all this means is that the ministry of preaching requires constant self-examination, which is perhaps one reason why the apostle James warns against it (James 3.1).

Finally, it is the habit of many preachers to tell stories about others, often their own families or friends or people they have encountered in ministry. I suggest that before telling stories about others there is one vital question we need to answer: do I have their permission? Clergy children especially suffer from this. They did not ask to be semi-public figures while they were growing up. So is it fair to use the sermon to put their growing up on display? Especially is this true if the story – perhaps of an incident as a young child – is potentially embarrassing to their mates, sitting on the back row or – even worse – listening later on the internet. For anyone whose story you want to use in a sermon, my rule would be: 'Always ask first.' Your spouse, children, relations and friends may be glad to give permission for you to use their story, but much less glad to hear about it being used without permission.

Providing 'handles'

Having used your introduction to grab the congregation's attention, to let them know exactly what the sermon is to be about and to suggest how best they can listen to it, how are you going to retain their attention all the way through to the conclusion? Oral communication is only heard once. Your listeners cannot go back, as they can when reading a book, to check on something they didn't quite pick up the first time. Nor can they go forward to find out how long there is to go!

There are other difficulties. An oral presentation moves in a single direction, one step at a time. People's thinking doesn't do this. While listening, people make connections of all kinds, which often mean that they become distracted. Moreover, you are limited in the speed you can speak, usually to no more than 100 words per minute. But people can think anything up to five times this fast. How then will you hold their attention and enable them to think along with you as you preach?

The answer is to communicate clearly where you are going. There are two ways to do this: *forecasting*, in which you let them know the points you are going to make at the beginning, and *unfolding*, in which you reveal your points step by step as you go along. The advantage of forecasting is clearly that it enables the listeners to work out how far you have to go as well as where you have already come. The disadvantage is that it conflicts with some of the structures you might want to use, especially if you also plan to make use of anticipation along the way.

Alvin Rueter tells the story of how initially he was sceptical of the need to provide 'handles' to signal his points as the sermon developed. That was until he enrolled in an undergraduate course on public speaking and found that both forecasting and unfolding were accepted without hesitation as essential ingredients of effective oral communication. When he tried the techniques out on his congregation, the result was that they consistently remarked on how much easier they found it to follow the sermon. Research suggests that it is at the transition points in a sermon that people are most likely to lose track of the preacher and let their attention wander. Rueter's experience suggests that the way to combat this is clearly to signal these transitions by summing up each point and providing a bridge to the next. He calls this 'underlining for the ear' and compares it with providing subheadings in a written piece of work (1997, pp. 93–8).

In the section on structure I wrote that structure is like a skeleton in a body: it holds everything securely in place but ought not to be noticeable. Don't forecasting and unfolding break that rule by drawing attention to the structure? Not necessarily: it depends how we go about it. Simply to say, 'My first point', 'my second point', 'finally' or 'lastly', especially if you repeat this week after week, is likely to lead to boredom and will certainly make the sermon sound wooden. But there are more artistic ways of going about it.

In my sermon on the sower, for example, the introduction closes with a statement of the message: 'The way you listen determines the way you live.' The next transition is into the first main section of the body, in which I want to set the scene for the parable. I might use two techniques to lead the listeners across this transition. First, I might pause to let the message sink in. A strategic pause in a sermon often has the effect of gathering people's attention, making them ready for whatever is coming next. Then I might begin the next section with an introductory sentence, clearly signalling what this section is to be about. I might say something like, 'Jesus encountered the same problem. Even though the things he had to teach the crowd were supremely important, he was aware that not everyone was listening.'

The first main section ends in the same way as the introduction, with a restatement of the message. So again a pause may be in order, to gather people's attention once more. And like the first, this second main section might begin with an attention-grabbing introductory sentence, perhaps referring to the radio programme *Beyond our Ken* and Kenneth Williams' catch-phrase, 'The answer lies in the soil.' Alternatively, I could introduce the next section with an explanation of what it is to be about: 'The farmer sowing his seed clearly hoped that as much of it as possible would grow and bear fruit, just as Jesus would have hoped for as many people as possible to listen and learn from his teaching. But the chances of the seed bearing fruit were clearly not random: they depended on the kind of soil in which the seed was sown. And the chances of people listening to Jesus, growing and bearing fruit were similarly predictable. It would depend on their attitude of heart.'

In my outline, the key to the third and fourth transitions are also clear. The third main section begins with a question: 'How can we become better listeners?' The conclusion begins by going straight into a story. But in each case a sentence or two to round off the previous section might help to signal this transition and take the listeners with me.

Exercise 3J

Use the passages you have already been working on in Exercises 3A, 3B, 3C and 3D.

At the head of the sermon, write down

- the message you want to convey in one sentence;
- your intention (to encourage, teach, warn, etc.);
- what you hope the response will be (a new perspective; a changed attitude; a definite action, etc.).

Now, prepare an introduction for the sermon. Use the following questions to guide you:

- How will you identify with the congregation?
- How will you put across the theme or message?
- How will you show them the relevance of the theme or message to them personally?
- What illustrations or stories might you use to make the theme more vivid?
- Will you introduce an element of anticipation and, if so, how?
- What will you ask them to *do* as you preach to help them to listen?

Note that you will need to prepare two versions of the introduction, one for a deductive structure, another for the alternative structure you decided on.

Exercise 3K

Look back at some of your sermons. Are there ways you could improve the introductions by following the guidelines in the previous exercise?

Exercise 3L

For the same sermons, are there ways you could provide better handles for the congregation to help them across the transitions? Aim to write a new passage for each major transition and compare it with your existing script to judge whether or not it is more effective.

Further reading

David Day, 1998. *A Preaching Workbook*. London: SPCK, Chapter 8: 'Faith, hope and clarity'.

Thomas G. Long, 2005. 'Pawn to king four – on introductions', in David Day, Jeff Astley and Leslie J. Francis, eds, *A Reader on Preaching*. Farnham: Ashgate.
Alvin Rueter, 1997. *Making Good Preaching Better*. Collegeville, Minnesota: Liturgical Press, Chapter 4: 'The risky but scriptural appeal to self-interest'; Chapter 7: 'Making homilies oral'.

Arriving at a conclusion

For many preachers the conclusion is the most difficult part of both preparation and delivery. Often, we resort to a simple 'Amen' or a piece of poetry, not knowing how best to close. Yet after the introduction the conclusion is one of the most important elements of the sermon. It is an intensification of the sermon as a whole, the place to draw together the strands of all we have planned to say and to leave the listeners with something memorable that expresses the message we hope to have put over.

So how do we know what a satisfactory conclusion looks like for any given sermon? How do we decide what to include? My suggestion is that the key to these two questions lies in intention and outcome, which is why deciding beforehand what these are is so important. If the intention behind your sermon is to teach, you will need a conclusion that summarizes and reinforces the message. If it is to challenge, you need to include elements that challenge, like a question or a challenging illustration. If it is to inspire, then the conclusion must focus on inspiration.

In the same way, knowing the outcome you hope for will also guide you as to what to include in the conclusion. In her sermon on the good shepherd, Julia Baldwin wanted to encourage her hearers to expect God's presence in the midst of pain and suffering. Her conclusion emphasizes that new perspective:

> *So* if the road of your life suddenly disappears into the sea, the fog descends or the panic sets in, trust the Psalmist with all your heart, soul and mind:
> Remember the good shepherd is active in your life – he might be the ferry that appears unexpectedly on the horizon or the chain underneath it all keeping you on course for dry land in a dark storm.
> Remember: 'even though I walk through the darkest valley',
> The Lord is *my* shepherd . . . the Lord is *your* shepherd . . . the Lord is *our* shepherd . . .

For his Advent sermon Tom Carson hoped for a definite action. He wanted the members of the two congregations for which he prepared the sermon to spend some time in reflection. Here is his conclusion:

> As you entered church this morning, you'll have been given a tea-light. This isn't for use in this service but is for you to take home with you. It should burn for over two hours, so will give you about five minutes each day between now and Christmas. If it helps you, take some time over these weeks to sit in silence with your tea-light burning and prepare yourself for Christ's advent . . .
>   Jesus is coming – look less busy.

The key then lies in intention and outcome. Whatever we decide to include in the conclusion should not only state the content of the message but fulfil the intention and promote the hoped-for outcome.

Below is a list of suggestions for the kind of thing you might decide to include in your conclusion depending on whether your intention is to teach, or to encourage, or to challenge; and whether your hoped-for outcome is a definite action, a new perspective or a change of attitude. But before listing these it is worth saying that, just as the elements of the introduction do not necessarily need all to come at the beginning of the sermon, so the things you choose to put in the conclusion do not all need to come at the end. The encouraging illustration, the challenging question, the call to think about one's own response and several more of these suggestions can, in fact, come at any point. The 'conclusion', in the sense of the reiteration and intensification of the message, may begin well before the end, before building to a climax in the closing section.

Here are the suggestions:

If your intention is to teach:

- A summary of your points
- A summary in the form: where we began – where we have arrived
- A restatement of the message in one sentence
- A sentence beginning, 'If you were only going to take one thing away . . .'

- A restatement, perhaps with illustration, of why the message is relevant
- A question to take away and think about.

And what the conclusion should *not* include is new information.

If your intention is to encourage:

- An apt quotation
- Use of humour to introduce a 'feel-good factor'
- A positive illustration from the church's past
- An optimistic prediction, or vision of what could be
- Placing the emphasis on possibility.

And all these will be reinforced by the preacher's tone of voice.

If your intention is to challenge:

- Give an example of what could be achieved.
- Pose a challenging question or series of questions.
- Give a challenging illustration.
- Use a parable.
- Share the way you, as preacher, are challenged.
- Use reversals and contrast, perhaps with words that jar.

These too will depend on the preacher's tone. In addition, it is important to be specific.

If you hope for a definite action:

- Provide a summary of the argument.
- Be specific about what you hope they will do.
- Offer a number of possibilities and ask them to decide.
- Tell a story of someone who took the hoped-for action.
- Give an invitation to try something for a week, or a month.
- Give a reminder that we are accountable to God.

If you hope to convey a new perspective:

- Summarize the argument of the sermon.
- Encourage people to recognize the possibility of thinking differently.
- Offer a contrast of perspectives and the consequences of each.
- Tell a parable.
- Ask the question, 'What has changed . . . ?'
- Give them a question to take away.

If you hope for a change in attitude:

- Be specific about what you are hoping for.
- Point to the benefits.
- Appeal to imagination.
- Include a warning.
- Ask a question.
- Offer a vision of the possibilities.

As we come to the end of this chapter, it is worth reconsidering the points made in the first chapter about the purpose of preaching. Preaching is about transformation: Jesus calls his disciples to live changed lives, lives that draw the attention of the surrounding community and bring glory to him. And the word of God is a powerful event that challenges and effects change. This poses the preacher a supremely important question. Do we really believe and desire that our sermons will make a difference in people's lives? Do we believe that, called and chosen by God for this ministry, we have the authority to challenge and inspire, to point people to the God revealed in Scripture and expect them to change as a result?

It is very difficult, if not impossible, either to prepare or to deliver a conclusion designed to challenge people if in your heart of hearts you don't believe that they are likely to be challenged, or don't believe that you have the right to challenge them. Even a desire to encourage people will lack conviction if you don't believe your sermon is likely to make a difference. But the very Scriptures from which we draw our messages week by week show God using ordinary flawed human beings to speak on his behalf and their words effecting remarkable change. Our authority to teach and inspire, encourage, warn or challenge is not our own. We do not earn it by our own expertise or erudition, or even through the quality of our lives. It is first and foremost God's gift and comes through his Holy Spirit. Our task is to live humbly under the 'weight' of this authority the kind of lives that reflect and sustain it; to give ourselves to study of the Scriptures and reflection on contemporary life and culture so as to be in the 'right place' to discern the message God wants us to convey; to love the congregation in such a way as to get a feel for the way each particular message can most effectively be conveyed.

Exercise 3M

Work with the sermon outlines you were using for Exercise 3J on introductions.

Add a conclusion, using the following as a guide:

- The conclusion should include a reiteration of your main message at some point, well signalled, i.e. 'underlined for the ear'.
- Ask what is the intention of the sermon (to teach, encourage, challenge, etc.) and include something that is aimed at achieving that intention: e.g. a question to consider, an illustrative story, words of encouragement, a reiteration of the main points, etc.
- Ask what is the intended outcome of the sermon (a new perspective, changed attitude, definite action, etc.) and include something that is aimed at encouraging that outcome. NB: this might be the same as whatever you have included for the intention, but be sure if this is the case – don't just be lazy!
- It helps the congregation to know that you are drawing to a close and that this is the conclusion: how will you signal that? Prepare fully the sentence or sentences that you will use to begin the conclusion.

Exercise 3N

See if you can draw up a list of possibilities for the conclusions of sermons whose intention is:

- to inspire
- to comfort
- to guide.

Some of these will overlap with the suggestions above, others may be distinct and different.

Further reading

It is remarkable how little is written specifically about the conclusion of a sermon. Perhaps this is because it really is the most difficult part!

4

Involving the congregation

Interactive preaching

Tim Stratford tells of the time he preached to a new congregation
for the first time. To help give him confidence, he had chosen an
existing sermon which had gone well on a previous occasion. But in
the new church it met only glazed looks. On reflection, he discovered
some of the reasons. The new church had a different culture from the
churches of his previous experience. He had been familiar with situations in which congregations were good at listening for 20 minutes
at a time and comfortable with the idea of the preacher as expert
with something to impart. In the new church, people tended to
feel 'put down' by experts. They were not so good at listening to
uninterrupted monologues, but what they did have was a lively sense
of community and a desire to give voice to their own thoughts and
feelings, including those about Christian faith and life (Stratford,
1998). In this situation interactive preaching, in which the congregation are encouraged actively to participate in the sermon, proved to
be a much more appropriate and effective means of building up the
church.

The world of communication is changing. In the early days of radio
and then TV, lengthy talks were common. Existing conventions of
communication had been transferred to the new media. But before
long, technological change began to transform the conventions of
communication. In the age of TV we have become used to visual
images, bite-sized items, dramatic interpersonal interaction, storylines
in which clear differences of opinion are easier to convey than nuanced
points of view and close identification with a range of people we may
never meet personally, from newsreaders to the characters in soap
operas. Perhaps most significantly, almost no programme on TV or
radio which involves a sharing of opinions fails to include an invitation for the audience to 'have their say'.

Meanwhile, the monologue sermon has continued with minimal change as the primary means of conveying God's word in the setting of worship. In some places, preachers draw on clips from film and TV and make use of PowerPoint, but without fundamentally changing the role and intention of the sermon as a one-way means of communication. Moreover, lacking the skill and resources to adopt the full range of innovation most of our congregations are familiar with, our use of these technologies can easily appear unskilled and second-hand.

While the church is unable to compete with television as a purveyor of mass entertainment or with the internet as a means of individually controlled, instant communication, its strength lies in the possibility of face-to-face community. In church there is an opportunity not only to establish friendships, something also offered by many workplaces, but to experience some things most workplaces cannot offer: the possibility of deeper interaction, the sharing of feelings and life stories, the exploration of values and deeply felt questions.

As the role of the Church in society has changed so too have the reasons people are drawn, or might be drawn, to church. Two generations ago the Church was a religious institution in a society moulded by institutions. As such, it possessed the authority expected of an institution. The sermon was a pronouncement made by a qualified and recognized expert. Since the 1960s, however, the authority of institutions has dissolved and the Church is still in the process of discovering a new role in a changed society. In a multi-cultural, pluralistic society, people no longer look to churches for authoritative guidance. Instead, what they look for are opportunities for exploration. In a fragmented culture, people are looking for 'wisdom for living' consisting of a set of values and practices capable of uniting the different, often competing aspects of their lives. And in a world of often broken and fraught relationships, many are looking for a safe place to share their pain and find healing.

Contemporary society is infinitely complex. These things are not true of all, and they tend to be less true of regular churchgoers, many of whom still welcome the traditional role of the Church as authoritative institution. For many of these the traditional sermon remains an accepted part of their spiritual diet. But for many others on the 'fringes of church', dipping their toes in the water, or who would like to do so, the traditional sermon is much less appropriate. Many may be kept away precisely because they do not see it as acceptable. The things people most want from a body claiming to communicate truth in an age of relativity and wisdom for living in an age of uncertainty include a non-judgemental welcome, the opportunity for exploration, honest face-to-face sharing and a safe place in which to unburden guilt and pain. Not only is the traditional monologue sermon completely unsuited to providing these, it may actually stifle them. We have to face the possibility that traditional sermons may already be inappropriate for parts of our culture and are likely to become increasingly so as time goes on.

Caveats

My intention in this final section is to encourage you to experiment with interactive preaching. But before going into detail about the reasons for doing so and suggesting some ways in, it is important to list some caveats: some reasons for *not* choosing to preach interactively.

First, there are many occasions when interactive preaching would be completely inappropriate and probably impossible. Since these include weddings, funerals, civic services and other occasions when the congregation includes a high proportion of visitors who may not be Christians, it is essential that we know how to preach interesting and inspiring monologue sermons.

Second, interactive preaching is not for every congregation. Some are comfortable with a traditional format and may know well how to listen and make the most of it. Equally, they may be profoundly uncomfortable being asked to venture an opinion, or share with those sitting around them. As Tim Stratford discovered, what works well in one culture may not go down at all well in another. In fact, some congregations seem to signal by the way they position themselves around the church that they definitely would not welcome an invitation to interact with their neighbours!

Third, it is vitally important to give people an opportunity to opt out. Almost every time I have paused in a sermon to ask people to think about a question and perhaps to talk about it with those sitting beside them, I have made it clear that this activity is strictly optional. No one is forced to do anything that would make them uncomfortable and no one will be put on the spot by being expected to speak.

Fourth, it is true that in a sense all good sermons are interactive. All good sermons will provide 'space' for the congregation to respond, even if only silently. A good sermon will evoke people's own experience and invite them to think about it in the light of the message. It will suggest ways of applying the message but leave these open-ended enough for the listener to decide what might be appropriate in her own case. It may provide an opportunity for the hearers to identify with one or more characters in Scripture, thus applying the text in a more direct and personal way than is possible simply through listening to the preacher alone.

Next, even in those churches where interactive preaching is possible and advantageous, it is not necessary to use interaction every time. There may be occasions when a straightforward monologue is a better option. Family services, Christmas, Remembrance and other special occasions may demand something different from the usual, but not necessarily the opportunity for interaction. Used too often, interaction may suffer from the same disadvantages as a particular sermon structure used without variation.

And finally, interaction requires a whole set of skills and attitudes *in addition* to those required to preach the traditional sermon. The following are just some of the most important:

- Skills in framing questions: the ability to choose the kinds of question required to evoke the response we are looking for from the congregation.
- Skills in facilitation: knowing how to encourage the timid and restrain the over-confident, how to respond to an obviously inappropriate contribution without discouraging the contributor or breaking the sense of community and shared exploration, how to cope with silence and turn it to advantage.
- Understanding of the sermon as a learning or exploring event, and with it the ability to match the activity we want the congregation to engage in to the right point in the sermon, balance the contribution of the congregation with our own as facilitator, and judge how much of our own 'voice' and our own insights as interpreters of Scripture, pastors and leaders are appropriate.
- Excellent knowledge of our subjects, in order to draw out a hesitant contribution, suggest links between one contribution and another, and draw together the various strands offered by congregational participation in order to provide a satisfactory ending to the sermon slot.
- The humility to recognize when the value of a congregational contribution is potentially greater for the occasion than the message we had hoped to convey.

Interactive preaching, then, is not to be lightly undertaken. In inexpert hands, in the wrong setting, or without serious thought and preparation, it is capable of going spectacularly wrong. Interactive preaching is a risk. But on the other hand there are many in our congregations who, I believe, are begging for us to take a risk of this kind, who long to go deeper in relationship with one another and in understanding and living their Christian faith. And although there are several caveats, there are some overwhelmingly good reasons for trying it out.

Why interactive preaching?

One reason is the limitations of the monologue as a tool for learning. Figure 4.1 (opposite) shows an overhead projector slide created by an adult education adviser who had stood at the back of a church after a service and asked members of the congregation what they thought the sermon had been about. The final contribution is that of the preacher himself. The sermon had not been particularly bad or confused but the quotations show a wide range of responses: some had taken away something valuable, even if it was not quite what the preacher had intended or hoped for; others were frankly bewildered and had made little of it. And without the adviser's intervention it is quite likely that the preacher would have been completely unaware how his sermon had been received.

There is a considerable body of evidence about the effectiveness or otherwise of the talk. Talks are useful for some purposes but not for others. They are a good way of confirming belief or reinforcing attitudes, which is why they are so often used in political gatherings. They are good at persuading the almost persuaded: drawing on a person's reflections on a particular subject and providing a conclusion or way of seeing. And they are equally as good though not better than other methods for giving straightforward information. But talks are not good when it comes to several of the purposes we might hope to achieve through our preaching: promoting thought, inspiring people to action or changing attitudes. For these, discussion and other interactive methods are far more effective.

A second set of reasons for looking beyond the traditional one-way sermon arises from the changes in culture and society that I mentioned in the opening section of this chapter. As we know, 'the medium is the message': the fact of the preacher in the pulpit or at

'About hurting people and how jealousy affects life'

'To reconcile my own place in the church in the context of evil in the world'

'The final words, "Don't be afraid of the world – don't let the world get you down"'

'Our way of living – my Christianity – how I live and share'

'About Jesus and the people who were listening to him'

'Never mind what's going on in the world today, think of God'

'It's difficult to remember'

'I get confused about Genesis – my mind goes blank'

'Can't really remember – something about why should terrible things happen'

'I didn't learn much for myself'

'That creation on its own is not all glory – the peace of creation comes through knowledge of Christ'

Figure 4.1 What was the sermon about?

the lectern preparing to speak without interruption conveys a message of its own, independent of anything the preacher may say. We need to ask what the format of the traditional sermon is telling us about the relationship between the preacher and the congregation. Is it really true that the preacher has all the expertise when it comes to Christian faith and life and the congregation has nothing to contribute? Is it really true that the Bible is the domain of experts, its message unclear until explained by one of the few who understand it properly? Is it really possible for one person to provide guidance in living the Christian life simply by explanation with examples? The danger of the one-way sermon is that, independent of anything the preacher says, it may incarnate all these false assumptions. In addition it may denigrate the value of the congregation's own experience and proclaim a church out of touch with the way people actually learn and grow in maturity.

There are some elements of the sermon in which the preacher is an expert by virtue of her training, others in which the congregation are the experts. The preacher, assuming she is properly trained, is an expert in the area of interpretation: she knows more than most if not all of the congregation about how to interpret the Bible and more about the Church's doctrines and practices. Yet even here I have sometimes been amazed by the insights into the meaning of Scripture brought by members of a congregation: far richer and certainly more varied than I had been able to discern in my prior preparation. And in the area of application it may not be the preacher but rather the congregation who are the experts. They are likely to know much more than the preacher about their own spiritual journey, the demands of their work or daily life situation, the history of their particular church and the character of the local community, while on the state of the wider world, the national and international issues in the news at any given time, preacher and congregation are likely to be equals. So while the preacher has valuable insights to share about the meaning of the Bible passage under consideration, it is wholly appropriate for the congregation to take an active part in discerning how to apply the passage to their everyday lives, their community and the wider world.

Interactive preaching affirms the spirituality of the congregation, encouraging them to value their own insights into Scripture and the Christian life. It recognizes them as active rather than passive learners, pilgrims on a journey of discovery together. It enables the preacher to learn from her congregation: about the problems they face in daily life and work, how they feel about their local community, what they value in the history of the church. In contrast, the one-way sermon disparages the congregation's knowledge, treating it as irrelevant or unimportant. It assumes an inability to grapple with the Bible unaided, and that the insights of the congregation into Scripture are less important than those of the preacher. Thus it inhibits or stifles completely the development of supportive community. Moreover it inhibits or even prevents the development of a local church as a 'community of interpretation' capable of offering a lively alternative to the assumptions of its wider culture.

Participatory preaching

So how does the preacher encourage and facilitate participation in the sermon? For most of us, especially at first, the answer will be: carefully and cautiously! First of all, here are some basic principles:

1 There is a spectrum as to the extent of congregational participation, depending on the amount of control you, as preacher, wish to retain. At one end of the spectrum is the typical 'family service' talk, in which most if not all of the questions are closed questions:

that is, they have a right or wrong answer. At the other is Doug Pagitt's concept of 'progressional dialogue' (2011), in which the preacher starts the topic off and then follows where the congregation leads. Therefore, before embarking on interactive preaching, you need to have an idea of how much control you want to retain and how much you are prepared to give away. Partly, this will depend on your own personality and experience. Mostly, I hope, it will depend on how much control you think is beneficial for your particular congregation and how much they are ready for, especially if participation in the sermon is likely to be unfamiliar and possibly threatening.

2 It may not be necessary to specify the content of the sermon as precisely for an interactive as for a traditional sermon, since you are prepared to allow the congregation to develop their own message to some extent. But for this very reason it is advisable to have a clear idea of the topic for the sermon. Without this, it is easy to allow congregational contributions to take the sermon in directions you have not planned for and a long way from the Scripture text, which may leave many of the congregation unsatisfied and even frustrated. It is still important for the sermon to end with a real sense of having grappled with a specific issue.

3 Likewise, your initial intention may have to be changed in the course of the sermon. For example, you may begin with the hope that the congregation would go away inspired, only for an unexpected contribution to include a salutary warning. Nevertheless, it is just as important as for the traditional sermon, if not more so, to have a clear sense of what God is doing right there and then as the sermon develops and to be ready to work with him.

4 Everything in the previous chapter about the structure of the sermon still holds good for interactive preaching. An interactive sermon requires introduction and conclusion, interpretation and application. It can also be structured deductively or inductively or be based around a narrative. This means that there is just as much work to do on the structure in preparation as for a traditional sermon.

5 Everything in the previous chapter about the power of concrete images also holds good for interactive preaching. But in an interactive sermon, the most powerful image may well be contributed by a member of the congregation, or it may occur to you, the preacher, in the course of the sermon as a way of drawing several contributions together.

Finally, it is important to bear in mind the stages of the learning cycle. A sermon is a learning event in which a congregation, individually or together, will encounter a biblical text, reflect on it, draw conclusions from it and think about how to apply it in everyday life and worship. When planning the parts of the sermon in which you want the congregation to participate, you need to be clear about the purpose of the task you are going to set them and where it fits in terms of the learning cycle.

It may be *to become aware of their existing mental model* of the subject of the sermon. Below are two examples. In the first, the reading was Matthew 5.13–16 with its images of God's people as salt and light. I wanted to challenge the congregation to consider the role of the church as light in its community. I drew on an interview with the playwright David Hare, who had just completed a play about a clergy team based on his experience not very far from the church where I was preaching:

A play recently began its run in the West End, called *Racing Demon*. It's about the lives of four clergymen in south London. Last month the writer David Hare described in a newspaper article his impressions of the priests he met while researching for the play. The article was entitled, 'Why I don't believe'.

> Hour after hour, day after day, there they were, out on the street, doing the most menial and demanding type of work. As they helped young couples to fill in DSS forms, or advised young blacks in trouble with the police, as they visited old people's homes or went to arbitrate on council estates, they served honourably as society's trouble-shooters, doing what was to all intents and purposes social work, and all on half of even a social worker's pay. But at no time did it seem part of their agenda to mention to the people they were helping that every Sunday, in another costume perhaps, they conducted services which related to a much-discussed incident in the Middle East 2,000 years ago.

David Hare is clearly expecting more from the clergy even than an outstandingly good sacrificial life. He wants to see a Church distinctively different from the rest of society with a cutting edge and the ability to proclaim what it believes – to stand up and be counted when it matters.

'The Church of England,' he says, 'looks like an organization which lacks the courage to set itself apart. It sounds too polite, too frightened,

> to remind us that its determining values are in fact radically different from those of the rest of society.'
>
> I'd like to invite you, as long as you are comfortable with this, to spend a bit of time discussing this question with the person next to you: 'Which church would you feel most at home as a member of: a polite, modest, sacrificial and well-meaning Church, or a radically different, outward-going, proclaiming Church?'

In the extract above I gave the congregation some stimulus material in the form of a very powerful quotation. The purpose was to help them to clarify what they already thought and also, in a sense, to get them to 'pin their colours to the mast' in conversation with their friends, before I went on to suggest why the church might need to 'own' and live up to Jesus' image of 'the light of the world'.

The sermon below is based on Ephesians 6.10–20 and the theme of spiritual powers. In this sermon, I started straight away by asking people to discuss their ideas about the powers of evil at work in the world. Again the purpose was to help people clarify what they already thought and I hoped also to gain confidence about their ideas through having these accepted and affirmed by those they shared with. My purpose then would be to build on these ideas. These are my notes:

> *Introduction*: Verse 12
> *Pairs*: Where do you think they do it?
>
> OHP feedback
>
> The life people lead is based on habits of thought
>   condition way people behave, choices, things think important
>   many deeply destructive people's happiness
>   spiritual powers spread wrong ways of thinking.
> This worldly attitude: previous generations people accepted
>   when we die we will give account of our lives to God
>   we need to prepare for death, make peace with God and others
>   I visit many whose relations have just died
>   rare that any have taken thought for life after death
>   this life only one; all matters live as long as possible.

Busy-ness: compulsion fill time with as much activity as possible
supermarket queuing: time to talk to neighbour? enjoy break?
race through traffic lights before red, save minute and a half.

Any others?

Another use of interactive activity is to *help the congregation to reflect on their experience.* You might ask people to share the feelings evoked when they see children being disobedient, or when someone at work is dishonest, or when they are praised by their friends. An exercise like this reminds us, as preachers, that people may not always feel the way we expect them to. Feelings are unique and help to make us who we are. But for this very reason, the opportunity to share feelings can draw a congregation together.

The invitation to share experience of the main theme goes deeper still. Here, you are opening the floor to personal stories and potentially to the experience of empathy and a shared experience of reflecting together. Here is one of the examples given by Tim Stratford in his Grove booklet (1998; italics in the original).

Sacrifices – for Passion Sunday

The preacher's hopes here were to connect with the feelings we have when we make small sacrifices for other people with what God was doing in the sacrifice of Jesus. In doing this we can discover a greater appreciation of God's love for us and can value our loving actions to others as echoes of our faith. The reading set was from Mark 10.

. . . The anticipated ice-breaker question was about the sort of sacrifices we sometimes make; the issue of substance for which there was to have been a more open space was about how we feel about some of the sacrifices people make. The assumption was that people would find it difficult to talk about their sacrifices. This was not to be. The sorts of sacrifices which had been anticipated:

- soldiers in war
- caring for children
- going to church
- giving presents

were small compared with the sacrifices actually shared by the congregation.

As in most churches, this was a place where everybody knew each other at one level and yet did not at another. Here a daughter with her elderly mother regularly sat at the front. After one contributor's brief and shallow mention of the sacrifices parents make for their children this particular young woman told the congregation very movingly about the sacrifices a daughter might make for her mother without the possibility of the mother growing up and leaving home. The mother joined in the conversation and told of the frustrations from her side. This was a most moving experience. In its liturgical context this conversation was safe in a way that it might not have been anywhere else. It led others to open up with real experiences of sacrifices too. We never just heard from a soldier who fought for king and country, but from a wife who had lost her husband fifty years ago and had never married again. There was no more incarnational entry into Passiontide than what this sharing offered. Later prayers of penitence and words of peace took on a new dimension across the congregation.

A safe conclusion that helped re-engagement with the liturgy, even though it was prepared in a relative vacuum, still had its place . . .

In the two examples immediately above, on spiritual powers and sacrifice, people were invited to share with the whole congregation. In the first example, on the church as light, I did not attempt this. In this case the reason was the size of the church and its layout, which would have made it virtually impossible for everyone to hear what was said. Factors like these will play a part in your decision as to how much participation is possible. Depending on the situation, it may be necessary or preferable to invite people to think quietly as individuals, to share only with one or two sitting either side of them, or to invite contributions for the whole congregation to hear.

Another stage of the learning cycle is the transition from conclusion to action, the application of what we have learned. I have argued that members of the congregation may have a much better idea of how to apply the message to their everyday lives than the preacher. Accordingly, another place for interaction in the sermon is *to provide the opportunity to share the perceived implications of the message.* In the sermon below I began in the traditional way by introducing the topic and then interpreting the Scripture passage, which was from 1 Corinthians 11.16-31, in which Paul writes about his tribulations. I then turned the application of the message over to the congregation.

Have you ever been driven to distraction by the people trying to serve
  but still loving them, still committed to their well-being
    still determined to go on serving and caring for them?
      those who are parents have some idea what I'm talking about!
2 Corinthians 10—13 this is Paul's situation
  church visited by preachers from Jerusalem
    flaunting their credentials, letters of commendation
      relying on impressive and powerful rhetoric
        manifestations of spiritual power
          spiritual gifts? Corinth high value; miracles of healing?
Arrogant, confident in outward signs of power and success
  Corinthian Christians same immature attitude
    presumed right to sit in judgement
      express preference for one over another.
How is Paul, as loving servant of Christ, to counter this?
  should he resort to same tactics as opponents?
    remind them of his success in founding churches?
      tell them about his extraordinary miracles in Ephesus?
        if he did, stepping down to level of opponents
          conceding Corinthians' right to judge him
            colluding with attitude of spiritual pride.
Rather than do this, he tries a different tack
  I'm going to boast, but not because I think boasting is a good thing
    but because you appear to require it
      and not of the most impressive aspects of ministry
        but the least impressive, the seeming failures
          'if I must boast, I will boast of things that show weakness'

ASK: how would you explain main theme of reading in one word?

ASK: can you give examples of situations like this today
      in ministry or in ordinary Christian discipleship?

ASK: how would you sum up the message of this passage
      to people facing situations we have talked about?

> *(Conclusion)*
> Weakness, set-backs, seeming failures
> are the things God uses to spread the gospel
> and draw us closer to him.

Each of the examples above is a way of mixing congregational participation with the preacher's role in exposition of the text. To an extent, some greater, some less, they are like traditional sermons punctuated with interaction. Tim Stratford's example comes closest to a sermon entirely built around interaction, and that appears to be because of the unanticipated power of what the congregation had to share.

It is equally possible to build the whole sermon around interaction, something already taking place in several 'emerging' new churches and 'fresh expressions' where the 'top-down' authority of the preacher as expert is rejected in favour of the preacher as facilitator. The following ideas are not necessarily drawn from such contexts but intend to provide a flavour of what might be possible:

Identify with a character in the story   Before reading the Scripture text for the 'sermon' invite the congregation to choose a person in the story with whom to identify. In some situations it may be better to divide the congregation into groups and allocate a character to each group, as I once did with the story of Jesus and the man born blind in John 9. One group were asked to identify with the disciples, one with the man himself, one with his parents and one with Jesus' critics. After the opportunity for discussion in pairs or small groups, there was an open invitation to share the insights that had arisen, and I was astounded by the depth and variety of what was shared, far richer than I could have achieved in solitary preparation.

Guided meditation   Begin by setting the scene for the story. At this point you, the preacher, are supplying a wealth of imaginative details: perhaps suggesting the mixed reactions at the wedding at Cana when the wine runs out, or what might be going on in the crowd gathered to hear Jesus teach but getting hungrier as the sun goes down. Members of the congregation could be invited to share their own responses, the feelings evoked or images that come to mind. The preacher then explains the particular text but rather than drawing her own conclusion invites the congregation to participate in the story again, perhaps with questions such as 'What would you say to Jesus?' 'How do you think he would respond?'

Godly Play   Originally devised for children, this form of responding to Bible stories can be equally applicable to adults. Like many of the methods we have looked at, Godly Play uses open questions to draw out the insights of all the participants rather than those of the preacher alone. Sam Wells in his chapter 'Imagination' uses Godly Play as one example of the power of imagination in a congregation.

Progressional dialogue   This is the method of preaching advocated by Doug Pagitt in his *Preaching Re-Imagined* (2005). In progressional dialogue the 'preacher' sets the ball rolling by outlining some thoughts on the text before inviting contributions from the congregation. Each contribution is intended to lead to another, with the aim that everyone listens carefully to one another and responds with respect to the insights and opinions shared. The preacher does not prepare the sermon in the sense of deciding beforehand what she wants to say, what the message and outcome will be. But she prepares by thinking carefully around the topic, knowing her own mind, but also the questions that may occur, the issues that might be connected. In a radical way, progressional dialogue trusts the Holy Spirit to speak through the congregation and trusts the congregation to listen to him through listening to one another. Before trying this, you should definitely read Pagitt's book. It is necessary to be entirely clear what you are aiming for in this form of 'preaching' and why you have chosen to do it.

Why preach?

In the same way it is necessary to be clear theologically about what you are doing if you invite a congregation to participate in the sermon. You will be introducing a different understanding of authority, one in which preacher and congregation stand together under the authority of Scripture and explore it together, rather than one in which the preacher stands between the Bible and the people. You will be requiring the congregation to listen to one another, thus inviting them to take the first steps on the road to becoming a 'community of interpretation'. You will be giving substance to the idea that worship involves the active participation of the whole people of God, rather than dividing the congregation between those with a part to play and those required to remain passive throughout.

Some congregations are not ready for such a transition, possibly never will be. But others are ready, and may only be held back by the reluctance or lack of confidence of their leaders. The decision to deconstruct a practice hallowed by tradition over hundreds of years is not to be taken lightly. On the other hand, perhaps the time is ripe. Perhaps the traditional sermon is an element of church culture as alien and irrelevant in our century as were the trousers and knives and forks introduced by missionaries overseas in the nineteenth.

Whatever the practice adopted in any particular situation, it must reflect the purpose of the ministry of the word in worship: to transform God's people into the kind of community God means them to become, to enable them to grow to spiritual maturity, to 'the measure of the full stature of Christ' (Ephesians 4.13).

Further reading

Jonny Baker, 2009. *Transforming Preaching*, Grove Ev86. Cambridge: Grove.

Donald A. Bligh, 2000. *What's the Use of Lectures?* San Francisco: Jossey-Bass.

John Drane, 2008. *After McDonaldization*. London: Darton, Longman and Todd.

David C. Norrington, 1996. *To Preach or Not to Preach: The Church's Urgent Question*. London: Paternoster.

Doug Pagitt, 2005. *Preaching Re-Imagined*. Grand Rapids, Michigan: Zondervan. Updated 2011 as *Preaching in the Inventive Age*. Minneapolis, Minnesota: Sparkhouse Press.

Tim Stratford, 1998. *Interactive Preaching: Opening the word and then listening*, Grove W144. Cambridge: Grove.

Sam Wells, 2008. 'Imagination', in S. Wells and S. Coakley, eds, *Praying for England*. London: Continuum.